BECOMING CHRIST

COWLEY PUBLICATIONS is a ministry of the Society of Saint John the Evangelist, a religious community of men in the Episcopal Church. Emerging from the Society's tradition of prayer, theological reflection, and diversity of mission, the press is centered in the rich heritage of the Anglican Communion.

Cowley Publications seeks to provide books, audio cassettes, CDs, and other resources for the ongoing theological exploration and spiritual development of the Episcopal Church and others in the body of Christ. To this end, it is dedicated to developing a new generation of theological writers, encouraging them to produce timely, creative, and stimulating publications of excellence, and making these publications available widely, reaching both clergy and lay persons.

BECOMING CHRIST

TRANSFORMATION THROUGH CONTEMPLATION

BRIAN C. TAYLOR

Published in the United States of America by Cowley Publications,
a division of the Society of Saint John the Evangelist. No portion of
this book may be reproduced, stored in or introduced into a retrieval
system, or transmitted, in any form or by any means—including
photocopying—without the prior written permission of Cowley
Publications, except in the case of brief quotations embedded in
critical articles and reviews.

Library of Congress Cataloging-in-Publication Data:
Taylor, Brian C., 1951–
   Becoming Christ: transformation through contemplation /
Brian C. Taylor.
       p. cm.
Includes bibliographical references
   ISBN 1-56101-200-9 (pbk. : alk. paper)
   1. Contemplation. I. Title.
   BV5091.C7 T38 2002
   248.3'4—dc21
                                                    2002005698

Scripture quotations are taken from *The New Revised Standard Version*
of the Bible, © 1989, by the Division of Christian Education of the
National Council of the Churches of Christ in the United States of
America. Used by permission.

Cover photograph: Tower of York Minster, by James von Minden,
SCC (Community of Celebration, Aliquippa, PA)
Cover design: Jennifer Hopcroft

This book was printed in the United States of America on acid-free
paper.

COWLEY PUBLICATIONS
907 Massachusetts Ave.
Cambridge, Massachusetts 02139
800-225-1534 • www.cowley.org

Contents

⚛

Acknowledgments

My deepest gratitude goes to:

The people, clergy, Vestry, and staff of my parish.
They allow me deeply into their lives as a priest,
generously encourage me to take the time to keep
my own faith alive, and fully support the work of
our Contemplative Center.

Cynthia Shattuck, who helped me clarify my
voice as a writer.

The Rev. Raymond Gunzel, s.P., who keeps
reminding me to trust the unfolding of the Spirit's
work in my life.

And always Susanna, whose loving and grace-
filled effect upon me is too great for words.

❆

Foreword

FOR SOME REASON there is a great interest in contemplation these days. Not everywhere, or even most places for sure, but enough to say that the Spirit is clearly moving human consciousness to both a new awareness and a new desire. I suspect that we have come to a "limit experience" as a species, and we know that somehow we need to break out and break through our limited ways of knowing. Yes, Descartes told us that "I think, therefore I am," but he never went on to say that this is also our major problem. Our identity is largely lodged in our cerebral thinking mode, and it has become our tomb. Contemplation, by whatever name you call it, has always been the way out of that tomb, and into a larger knowing that we Christians might call "the mind of Christ" and others might call enlightenment.

Brian Taylor is doing us a great service in providing such a clearly written, profoundly ancient, and yet contemporary basis for this larger knowing that we now call contemplation. If you are a beginner—and aren't we all—you will find a solid foundation here. If you are wanting to go further, there is enough good material here, to build a second or third floor of wisdom. This is not just spirituality, which is "in" now, but even, dare we say it, the wisdom of the Holy Spirit.

I am more and more convinced that the gift of the Holy Spirit is precisely the gift of a contemplative stance and a contemplative presence toward life. Just look at John 14, and within ten packed verses hear the rich metaphors that he offers: "advocacy," "truth," "with you, in you," "un-orphaned," "I live and you will live," "knowledge of indwelling," "showing Myself to you," "making our home in you," "teaching you everything," "reminding you of all," "the peace the world cannot give," "which is my own peace," so "do not be troubled." These are not metaphors that feed the intellect, but images that *only* make sense inside of the contemplative mind which is larger than intellect. They *come* from the contemplative mind and easily *return* there. In fact, they describe, excite, and satisfy anyone who has tasted this larger knowing. They are the language of Presence which only makes sense to presence, but not to thinking.

My suspicion is that our undeveloped theology of the Holy Spirit largely explains our undeveloped attraction to and practice of contemplative prayer. As long as we thought we had to do it all by technique, asceticism, and years of withdrawal, most of us gave up on contemplation and left it to the supposed monks and nuns somewhere. Sadly, we found out that most of the monks and nuns had lost touch with the tradition too. They were often "saying" prayers but had not always been led to that new home, that un-orphaned state, where Someone else is praying in us, through us, and with us. They had not always "become" prayer, which is the real meaning of contemplation. Someone else is our Advocate. And all we can do is allow. And thank. A Holy Spirit was always given but seldom recognized. Like Jacob at the foot of the ladder, we find ourselves awaking from sleep and saying, "You were always in this place and I never knew it" (Genesis 28:16). Now this book, like the Spirit, will "remind" you.

So I will not belabor what does not need belaboring and what the Spirit is already doing. I will only add my small encouragement to Brian Taylor's excellent presentation and to the encouragement from the centuries that he offers in these pages. This is good fare for all of you who are no longer orphans and even more, for those who no longer want to be.

Fr. Richard Rohr, O.F.M.
Center for Action and Contemplation
Albuquerque, New Mexico

❁

Part One: Practice

FOR SOME, THE TERM CONTEMPLATIVE PRAYER may be intimidating. Perhaps when you think of contemplation, you envision pious, holy mystics who are lost in rapture. While a few such saints have always existed (and many of them have been contemplative), there are other ways of being contemplative that are far more ordinary. Silent prayer that has no other purpose than to be present to God is contemplative.

I assume that because you hold this book in your hands, you are attracted to this way of being with God. I do not assume that you are experienced in it. But even if you are, my hope is that you will benefit from what I have to say about my experience with contemplative prayer. I share with you here a particular approach which I have learned over years of practice. I suggest that you try it long enough to know in your own experience what I am talking about, instead of reading about it simply out of curiosity.

We begin with instruction and discussion about the doing of silent prayer. Before we talk about what it means or where it leads, it is best to just pray, and see for ourselves what happens. The first chapter in this section presents a practical instruction and orientation to the kind of contemplative prayer with which I work. The second chapter goes into more depth about how we can pray contemplatively with our whole being, and the third suggests ways of praying contemplatively in Christ.

One

❈

Getting Started

ALL OF US ARE POTENTIALLY CONTEMPLATIVE. What may be called a "contemplative experience" is natural and common to most of us, at least once in awhile. We are struck dumb by massive shafts of sunlight breaking through dark thunderclouds, falling on the desert. A sleeping child on our lap makes us completely still and fills us with utter peace. In a moment of extreme suffering something opens up and we somehow know that even though everything is "wrong," everything is really all right; a confrontation by someone who loves us leads us to quiet, deep, honest surrender. In one way or another, we find our way into stillness, quiet, a full emptiness; we open to a place within that is truthful, grounded, humble, and utterly real.

Or perhaps it would be more accurate to say that the contemplative experience finds its way into us. For contemplation itself is a gift from God; it is not an accomplishment of our own.

Some, perhaps most, are satisfied with this occasional gift of peace and openness, knowing that they cannot control or manufacture it. Others of us want more. We sense that what we glimpse in moments is more vital and alive than our usual mode of being, which can be so attached and self absorbed. We feel called to seek out this deeper, simpler, truer reality through prayer and meditation, so that our occasional glimpses might come more often and be more sustained. And so we are drawn into some form of prayer that promises to ground us in stillness, vitality, and peace. For many of us, this form of prayer is silence.

Once we begin to invite God's presence into our silent prayer, the Spirit within takes our desire seriously, and guides us forward into the divine presence. We are led into a loving and life-changing relationship with God. For ultimately, prayer, any kind of prayer, is a relationship with a personal, loving God.

In this relationship of prayer, I believe that God wants to awaken us to joy for the divine life within and around us; to help us respond to this presence by becoming people of loving compassion; and to come to complete honesty about everything in us that stands as an obstacle to this joy and love. Through a life of prayer, over time, we are transformed.

The Spirit shows some of us how we grasp compulsively at life and then helps us become more patient and accepting; God reveals to perfectionists just how self-condemning they are, and then teaches them forgiveness and their inherent worth as children of God. Others of us are shown our self-centeredness so that we can move beyond it into compassion and service to others. As we devote our hearts to God in prayer, and as the Spirit brings us to self-awareness in that relationship, we grow more fully into the persons God has created us to be.

This spiritual growth is the whole point of a life of prayer: not to attain and sustain pleasant or deep "spiritual" experiences for ourselves, but to be transformed by God into a more perfect fulfillment of the persons we are created to be.

As Christians, there is an ideal towards which we are aimed in this transformative fulfillment. This ideal is Christ, whom we are called to become. This may sound like a bold and ambitious claim, but it is our traditional hope that Jesus came to show us the nature of both God and humanity, at its best, in order that we might allow him to live his life through us. As St. Paul said "it is no longer I who live, but it is Christ who lives in me" (Gal. 2:20). Through the transformation that takes place in the relationship of prayer, we become less dominated by our attachments, fears, and other habitual ways in which we limit ourselves, and we become more like Jesus Christ. What is this Christly life like?

Jesus promised a quality of life to his followers, which he called the kingdom of God, or the kingdom of heaven. This quality of life is marked by unconditional love (especially for the powerless), forgiveness, peace, honest encounters with evil and injustice, healing, and freedom from all kinds of captivity. As we live into our Christly identity, we experience this kingdom more and more; we experience Christ's life in us to a greater degree. Prayer helps us in this regard, and contemplative prayer does so in an intensified way. It moves us into the kingdom that Jesus promised; it helps us to become Christ.

An example from my own life may help illustrate this transformation. I grew up with a fear that arose out of an unexamined conviction that if I did not make sure that things went my way, I would not get what I wanted. The result was that I spent an enormous amount of time subtly manipulating events and people, planning everything out, imagining and worrying about future possibilities. All of this was, for the most part, unconscious, but it dominated my mind, my emotions, and my actions. It controlled my life. As such, it was an obstacle to God, a hindrance to the kingdom of which Jesus spoke so often. This was the specific way in which I attempted to control life and thereby shut out God's freedom and joy.

Eventually, as I began to sit in contemplative silence, I began to see and experience quite clearly what I was doing. In the relationship of love that is prayer, God brought to light those habits of mind and heart that I was using in order to deny the kingdom of heaven in my life. My own process of "becoming Christ" was a transformation wherein God brought to my awareness those patterns that stood in Christ's way. Over time, these habits melted in the light of awareness, and there was more room for Christ to live in me, more freedom where I could experience the kingdom of heaven, more equanimity.

There are many ways of opening ourselves to this Christly transformation. This fact allows all of us with different temperaments and callings to find a way that works for us. Some are best suited to verbal, interactive prayer: they talk to God, read scripture, ask questions and seem to receive answers. Others are most affected by liturgical prayer: for them, the heart of their devotion is experienced in the eucharist or other corporate worship. Still others find prayer in activity, relationship, in everyday duties: their hearts are most open to God when they are talking to others, working in the garden, or taking a walk.

Contemplative prayer is *not* the best, highest, and "most spiritual" path to God. It is simply the best way for some of us. If you find that you have run out of words, that you must be still, and that you cannot pray as well otherwise, then perhaps contemplative prayer is your path.

By the same token, there are many approaches to contemplative prayer itself. Some approaches are more devotional than others and use words in order to lead one into wordless prayer. *Lectio divina* is an example of this, where one takes a passage of scripture and meditates on it, prays about it, then enters into silence. Other forms of contemplative prayer include meditative walking, such as the use of a labyrinth. Some methods of contemplation emphasize complete stillness and an emptying of the mind; others place attention on an opening of the heart in love, such as devotion to the Sacred Heart of Jesus; some develop concentration using a repetitive mantra; others maintain a more open, fluid atmosphere.

Centering prayer, as advanced by Thomas Keating and others, is especially popular in our day. Its focus is upon "letting go" of thoughts as they arise, and gently but insistently keeping the intention of prayer focused in loving attentiveness towards God. This particular approach works well for many, especially as a beginning point for learning how to be quiet and detach from the mind's relentlessly gripping activity. But centering prayer is not the only form of contemplative prayer, and it is not the best path for everyone.

There is no formula, no absolute recipe that is the "right" way for everyone to pray. In talks given to monks under his care, Thomas Merton reminded them that the work of contemplative prayer consisted not so much

> in a secret and infallible method for attaining to esoteric experiences, but in showing us how to recognize God's grace and his will, how to be humble and patient, how to develop insight into our own difficulties, and how to remove the main obstacles keeping us from becoming [people] of prayer....in the spiritual life there are no tricks or shortcuts.[1]

Contemplative prayer, then, is a gift from God, for which we prepare ourselves by sitting in silence and inviting the work of the Spirit within us. It is a relationship wherein we seek God's loving trans-formation, and develop insight about our own obstacles to this transformation. No method will guarantee its attainment, and there is no easy, quick route that will take us there.

The approach I take in this book is a specific one, and it will work for some, but not for everyone. As may be already evident in these few pages thus far, underlying my approach is a primary assumption that contemplative prayer involves two essentials: worship of God and self-

---

1 Thomas Merton, *Contemplative Prayer*. (Garden City, NY: Image Books, Doubleday, 1971), 36–37.

awareness. The first leads us deeply into God, the second into ourselves. Worship opens us up to a divine reality that transcends all our concerns and problems; self-awareness helps us encounter and heal all our habitual patterns that block spiritual growth and fulfillment.

What follows, then, is a simple and practical introduction to prayer that is based upon this basic assumption. My hope is that you will either begin practicing this approach or adjust your current practice of prayer to what I suggest, so that as you continue to read the rest of the book, you will understand more fully what I present, because of your own experience with it.

Even though I present a kind of "how-to" in the pages that follow, please understand that prayer cannot be reduced to a method. If it could, we would be able to control its outcome. Prayer is a relationship with the living God, who will both guide and surprise us. The instruction I offer, therefore, is given simply as a concrete example of the general approach to a contemplative relationship with God that I have found to be not only beneficial, but life-changing. Some elements of what I present will be more appropriate than others at times. Some parts of it will not be possible until other parts are in place. But since no one can predict where another person will find themselves as they begin to pray, there is no step-by-step order that will "work." One size does not fit all.

Some of you will find that as you begin to enter into silence, you experience a quiet, open stillness, at least at first. Others may find yourselves caught up in endless chains of free-associative thoughts, unable to rise above them into any kind of inner silence. Still others might discover, despite your best intentions, that you cannot help planning, worrying, imagining, or entertaining yourselves.

Because of the limitations of writing, I must present different components of this approach in some kind of order. But keep in mind that the order in which they are presented may not be the right order for you. It is an overview of different aspects of contemplative prayer, each of which may be discovered, needed, and employed at different times.

And yet, in spite of this encouragement to be flexible, we must also learn to commit ourselves to a specific practice, for a spiritual dilettante will always be self-limiting. Only by undertaking particular disciplines over time do we reap the benefits they promise. It is my hope that if the approach represented here speaks to you, you will daily undertake its discipline in your life, be guided by the Spirit in your prayer, and be provided with whatever support and insight you need in order to sustain your practice over time.

First, I will begin with an outline of the overall approach I offer, so that you will know where I am headed. This outline may also serve as a handy reference when you want to refresh your memory about it. Following this brief outline, I will provide some commentary on each of its components.

- Begin with body awareness, silence, stillness.
- After settling into silence, ask the Spirit (or Christ) to assist you in prayer.
- Find a way of "warming" or "softening" the heart towards God.
- Establish the use of an occasionally repeated word or phrase that expresses an open intention in prayer, saying it silently, whenever needed, to bring yourself back to attention.
- Open your heart towards God, maintaining a light, spacious, empty awareness.

Dealing with involuntary thoughts that arise in prayer:
- Sometimes passing thoughts arise that do not affect openness and the ability to be present in the moment: look past them to God.

- Sometimes other more compelling or passionate thoughts momentarily capture the attention, closing down the open awareness to a narrow focus: notice the thought, name it and then return to the use of your word or phrase.
- Sometimes an emotionally and physically charged or obsessive thought persists: simply feel its energy physically, stay with it as long as it lasts, and make this awareness your prayer.

Close the time of contemplation with a prayer of thanksgiving and dedication.

Begin with body awareness, silence, stillness.
Sitting upright with a straight spine, keep eyes partly open and the gaze fixed on a point in front of you; remain as still as you can throughout the time of prayer, without shifting around. Pay attention to the breath, to your body, to the world around you through your senses.

As Christians, we have historically been quite negligent about the role of the body in meditative prayer. For this reason I will, in this instruction and commentary, spend quite a bit of time on the details of physical posture. Contemporary Christian prayer group members lean against walls, lounge in easy chairs, cross their legs, move and look around. Then they wonder why they cannot maintain stillness, why their backs gets sore, and why they do not experience the integration of mind and body as one, centered entity.

Hindus and Buddhists have experimented and refined the physical demands of sitting meditation far more than we. What they have developed, over many centuries of practice, are some principles that are fairly easy to maintain. They are important, not because physical posture has anything to do with holiness, but because they increase our ability to sit still, with attention and comfort, for long periods of time.

The back should be straight. The body, even though erect, should not be rigid, but relaxed. Imagine something gently pulling your skeletal framework upwards, with your muscles loose and unengaged. It is a balance of alertness and gravity. Whether you are in a chair or on a cushion or on a kneeling bench, it does not matter. This principle still holds for any posture. If you are physically incapable of sitting up, you can lie flat on your back on the floor, with the knees bent and feet flat on the floor, eyes focused on the ceiling. If even this is not possible for you, just find a position that allows you to remain still for a period of time.

In order for the back to be straight when sitting, one should either be in a straight-backed chair (not an easy chair), on a kneeling bench, or on a meditation cushion. If it is a cushion, make sure it is a firm meditation cushion, not a few soft pillows. For those who sit on the floor, a cushion is essential (rather than sitting right on the floor or a flat mat) because it raises the seat up above the legs, which are crossed. This tilts the pelvis slightly forward.

Whether you are in a straight-backed chair, or on a kneeler or a cushion with the seat raised up and the pelvis tilted forward, the effect should be that there is a slight arch in the lower back. This puts the spine into alignment. Alignment helps us maintain an alert, relaxed posture for long periods. Without this natural, relaxed, erect position of the spine, you will not be able to remain completely still, the back will become sore, you will have to move around or collapse into a rounded position, and your mind will also collapse into distraction and sleepiness.

The neck and head should be in line with the spine, not sticking out in front or leaning back. I believe it is best for the eyes to be open, and the gaze fixed on one spot 45 degrees in front of you. Some discover that having the eyes open really does not work for them, but the advantage (if it does work) is that it helps keep you awake and centered in this present, ordinary moment, and less likely to go off on some imaginative internal tour. Others, however, find less distraction by closing their eyes. Your hands should be on your lap, fingers uncrossed, or on your thighs or knees.

If you are on a cushion with crossed legs and one knee is higher than the other, the higher knee should be supported by a small cushion. Whether in a chair, bench, or cushion, the overall sense should be that you are grounded in gravity through the parts of your body that carry your weight: seat, and knees or feet. And remember, keep this gravity balanced with a gentle upward pull of the skeletal structure, from the head down through the spine. The chest should be open, with the shoulders comfortably back (not arched).

Complete stillness is important because it helps us remain with whatever is happening, rather than moving our attention around in a distracted manner. It forces us to be present in a way that shifting around does not. When we move, however subtly, we are giving our bodies and therefore our mind a little escape hatch. In doing so, we are giving in to the silent suggestion that since this moment is getting boring or difficult, it might just be a little better or easier if we just moved ourselves physically and mentally a little bit. This subtle suggestion is the same as other subtle distractions in our lives: just a little bit of ice cream, a glass of wine, a few minutes with the television, a little cleaning up here and there....all in the vain hope that some little shift will give us relief, entertainment, something new and better. We may spend our entire lives not being present, shifting around a little here and there in the hope for something a little better.

This may seem like a fine point, but I believe that sitting completely still in prayer is essential, so that we learn how to be completely dedicated to remaining present with whatever the moment brings. As we sit still, we learn that we can tolerate, and learn from, far more than we think we can. Complete stillness helps us move to another level of presence that is not possible without it. It also leads to an integrated, peaceful silence that pervades mind, heart, and body.

At the same time, it must be recognized that this is not a machismo contest. If you are in persistent physical pain and this pain has the potential to do some real damage, by all means, move to a position that is better. But what this says, if it continues, is that you have not yet settled in to a position that works for you. Anyone should be able to discover, over time, a position that keeps the back straight, the body alert and relaxed, and that is possible to hold in complete stillness for at least a half an hour. Avoid shifting around, avoid even scratching yourself (just feel the itch: it will pass).

Once you are in this position, begin with attention to the breath for a few moments. Do not manipulate it: just watch and feel it. Similarly, move your attention to your body, doing a brief scan from top to bottom, pausing in each location to feel any sensations that might be there. Bring particular awareness to any part of the body, at any point in your time of prayer, that is tight. Focused awareness tends to relax the muscles involved.

Then move your attention outside the body to the room around you. Feel the air on your skin. Listen to the sounds that occur and accept them as part of your landscape for the moment. Without moving your eyes, take in everything visually, including in your peripheral vision.

The reason for bringing awareness to the posture, to the breath, the body, and the senses is to root our whole being as children of the earth. This has the effect of centering us in reality, rather than in our minds alone. Moving from this place of grounded, earthy awareness, it is more possible to pray in an integrated way.

After settling into silence, ask the Spirit (or Christ) to assist you in prayer.
Simply say something like "Lord, you know that I desire you but without you I cannot even pray. Guide me. Pray through me."

Whatever happens in prayer, we must trust that God is the primary agent. We are simply doing what we can, always imperfectly, to open ourselves to God's grace, which works in a way that is usually hidden to our mind.

It is important to examine our intention. What do we really want? To feel peaceful? To learn something? To let go of and not be troubled anymore by something that bothers us? There is nothing wrong with specific intention in prayer, but contemplative prayer usually works best without any intention beyond self-offering. After all, perhaps God wants us to be troubled or confused awhile longer so that we can get to a place that is necessary for real transformation. In our prayer of intention, then, we simply pray that God, who is already completely present within and around us, will do whatever needs to be done in this time of prayer.

This invitation is important, because it cooperatively unites our own God-given personal will with God's grace. As we look at the record of scripture and the lives of the saints, this cooperation is essential. God will not work without our invitation. Jesus said, "Ask and it will be given to you, search and you will find, knock and the door will be opened" (Luke 11:9), but we must ask, search, and knock. God does not jump into our lives uninvited. At least not usually.

And so our prayer of dedication opens a door; it establishes the needed connection between our desire for God and God's desire for us. As such, our personal longing, which seems very important to God, joins forces with the energy of God's Spirit, who awaits our invitation.

It is important to recognize our need for God's assistance even to pray, as Paul said: "The Spirit helps us in our weakness; for we do not know how to pray as we ought, but that very Spirit intercedes with sighs too deep for words," (Romans 8:26). We cannot even manage decent prayer for a few minutes without going off into some silly or self-centered fantasy. A spiritual giant no less than Teresa of Avila is reported to have said that fifteen minutes of prayer is fourteen minutes of distraction. We need God's help just in order to pray. To ask for this help is also a reminder, again, that prayer is God's work in us more than it is our work. In prayer we learn to trust the hidden movement of the Spirit, sighing within us in a way that is deeper than words, bringing us into the presence of God.

As Christians, our life of prayer must be, in one way or another, Christ-centered. One way of doing this is to ask Jesus for the assistance needed before beginning prayer. As the human face of God, he is the one who takes us into the experience of love and unity that he enjoys with the Father. You might begin with a brief prayer of dedication that acknowledges his presence and asks him to guide you during your time of prayer in ways that are consistent with his life, his way. For this purpose it may be helpful to pray in the presence of an icon of Jesus.

Find a way of "warming" or "softening" the heart towards God.
Recall something about which you feel deeply, or bring to mind your longing and desire for God, your gratitude, or an awareness of sin: anything that will make you vulnerable before your Creator.

Remember that in prayer, you are in the presence of God. This is no small, casual encounter that we can blithely skip in and out of. It is, if it is to be effective, an encounter with the source of our being, with the very source of life and death. Keeping this in mind, as the early desert and Eastern monks taught, we must become humble, vulnerable, and open before God by "warming" or "softening" the heart. What did they mean by this?

We know that when real communication about something important must occur between two people who love one another deeply, they must get to a place of honesty that arises out of vulnerability. So it is with God. This should not be artificially manufactured in our time of prayer, and certainly we cannot expect a big, heartfelt opening of the floodgates every times we pray, but there is something to this that is crucial to prayer.

As we carry ourselves through the day, we normally maintain subtle defenses, just in order to cope with everything we must do and everyone we must relate to. In prayer, we must drop these defenses and stand naked before God. But it is not always easy to do so immediately. This is why it may help to call to mind something that lies beneath your defenses: a sharp awareness of your sin; a grateful sense of joy; the intense longing you feel for God's presence; the painful concern you feel for someone whom you love who is in need.

The Eastern Orthodox contemplative tradition of the prayer of the heart, which has been sustained over fifteen hundred years by monks around the Mediterranean as well as in Russia, has a well-developed sense of the importance of this practice. They not only recommend a "softening" of the heart as I have described, even to the point of weeping and feeling physical warmth in the chest, but also a concentration of our attention in prayer upon the physical and spiritual heart, the center of our being. I will say more about the prayer of the heart later, but for the purpose of this instruction, the following brief description will do for now.

Place your concentration, your awareness, in the center of your chest. This physical center of your body represents the very center of your whole being, the "place" where you have your deepest encounter with the

Spirit, with Christ. Keeping your attention fixed there, feel your breath causing your chest to expand and contract; feel your heart beating. Feel the heart, which has been made "soft" and vulnerable to God through joy, contrition, or desire. Remain in this place, feeling your breathing, your heartbeat, your openness to the One who is already present in this very place within you. You may, as the tradition suggests, even feel a certain warmth around your heart as you do so.

The nineteenth century Russian Bishop Ignatii Brianchaninov speaks of the effects of bringing the mind's concentration into the heart:

> Before long the heart begins to be in sympathy
> with the attention of the mind as it prays. Little
> by little the sympathy of the heart with the mind
> begins to change into a union of mind and heart.[2]

Establish the use of an occasionally-repeated word or phrase that expresses an open intention in prayer, saying it silently, whenever needed, to bring yourself back to attention.
From time to time say "Opening to you," "Jesus, have mercy," "Thank you," "Open my heart," "Here I am," or even "Opening," "Heart," or "Jesus." Try to avoid such words as "peace," "joy," or other descriptions of desired moods, as this can be a form of emotional self-programming.

The purpose of using a word or brief phrase occasionally in our times of prayer is to provide our minds with a sort of re-start button. As we drift around mentally, the quiet re-introduction of a word or phrase brings us back to center. Use it only occasionally, when it is needed in order to return to an empty openness to God in the moment.

---

2 *The Art of Prayer*, compiled by Igumen Chariton, trans. E. Kadloubovsky and E.M. Palmer, ed. Timothy Ware (London: Faber and Faber, 1966), 104.

This word or phrase should not be directive in nature, but open in its intention. Its use is not an attempt to program one's thinking or feeling towards a desired outcome. It is a way of staying open and present to whatever the moment brings, a way of expressing our need and desire for God from time to time. In this way we remind ourselves, as needed, just what we are engaged in as we sit in silence: a loving attentiveness to our Creator.

In the discipline of the prayer of the heart, the phrase that is normally used is what has come to be called the Jesus Prayer. Its words are "Lord Jesus Christ, Son of God, have mercy on me, a sinner." The tradition has allowed for, even encouraged, a shortening of this phrase, so that one might say "Lord Jesus Christ, have mercy on me," or "Jesus, have mercy," or even just "Jesus." In this tradition, the name of Jesus is always a part of the phrase, in order to call upon the One in whom we live, and by calling upon him, invoke his presence and power in our lives.

The Jesus Prayer can be used, as I suggest, as an occasional spiritual "re-start" only when needed. But more commonly, it is said repetitively, over and over, not only throughout the entire period of formal prayer, but also throughout the day, or at least from time to time when we think of using it. As such, it becomes a kind of familiar track upon which the mind can run, directing us quickly to God.

The use of the Jesus Prayer, or any other brief phrase directed to God, as a constantly-repeated mantra can be extremely helpful for beginners as a way of developing concentration during an intentional time of silent prayer. Some find that when they begin to enter into silence, they are overwhelmed by a constant barrage of thoughts and fantasies. It is impossible to pray, it is impossible to stop the thoughts, and it is impossible to sort them out or see any space between them. One thought leads into another through free-association so quickly and fluidly that by the time we're even aware that we have been caught up in thinking, we have moved through several linked thoughts in a short space of time.

If this is the case, then use the Jesus Prayer or some other phrase or word as if you are holding on to a lifeline. Repeat it over and over, uniting it with the breath. Without artificially speeding up or slowing down your breath, say "Lord Jesus" on the inhale, "Have mercy" on the exhale. Use a set of prayer beads if that helps, moving the fingers from bead to bead each time you breathe and repeat the phrase. In this way the body and mind are united in prayer, assisting your concentration.

Keep bringing your mind back to its words and slowly develop the capacity for better concentration. Over time the thoughts will slow down, and gradually you will even be able to see open spaces between and around them. You will then be less of a victim of your thoughts, carried against your will wherever they want to take you. Only at this point will the section following that deals with involuntary thoughts make much sense or be useful. For it is not possible to ignore, notice, step out of, objectify, or name thoughts if you are just carried along by them in a completely unconscious way.

Open your heart towards God, maintaining a light, spacious, empty awareness.
Without words, just feel—with your breath, your open heart, your mind, your whole being—that you are awake, expectant and attentive to the moment in God. Use your word or phrase as a kind of spiritual "re-start" button when needed.

As long as you are awake and open in the moment, unhindered by gripping thoughts and distractions, enjoy it! Sometimes the silence and the stillness is complete and uninterrupted, in which case the use of a word or phrase is quite unnecessary. Just be still, open, and direct your loving attention towards God.

This empty openness before God is worship. It does not require any specific direction or content beyond just being with God. This kind of worship is the simplest and most faith-based form of prayer, for it only asks us to be present, in complete trust. We do not trust that anything measurable or discernable will happen; we just sit in God's presence, having the faith that God will use the time of prayer in a way that is most needed for us. Even if we do not see or feel the results of this kind of prayer, we trust that something is happening, that the Spirit is working within our trust and our willingness to be open.

But to really trust in this kind of prayer, we must come to the point where we know that prayer is God's work in us even more than it is our work. We come to prayer, invite God's presence, open our hearts, and cooperate with God's action through our willingness to be present. The rest is up to God. And even though we might not see any "benefit" to this prayer, we learn to trust that spiritual work is taking place, by the action of the Spirit.

Prayer, after all, is so much more than our effort; it is so much more than us and our experience. Prayer is also the divine presence of the living God. Contemplative prayer takes this seriously, trusting in something we cannot see or feel. Healing, insight, transformation, enlightenment: all of this is the work of God, not our accomplishment, and it really does take place, over time, in the prayer of faith. Our job is to be available, to wait.

And so the times that we simply sit in quiet, with an open heart and a faithful intention, we are doing all we need to do in prayer. It is enough to enjoy this kind of time with God, to move out of our obsession with getting things done, and trust that something is taking place in the peace and quiet.

However, anyone who has spent some time in silent meditation or prayer knows that this state of peaceful availability is not something we can just conjure up or maintain out of sheer will power. The mind has a mind of its own. Distractions arise and persist, taking us out of that peaceful place of presence in God.

How do we deal with distractions? Many teach the practice of "letting-go" of all thought, and there is benefit to this practice; it helps us learn to concentrate, to stay focused with our simple intention to be present. I am going to propose another way. This way recognizes that if we objectively observe the content of involuntary thoughts, we come to a profound and accurate self-awareness, and through self-awareness to healing and transformation in God.

Dealing with involuntary thoughts as they arise in prayer

Sometimes passing thoughts arise which don't affect openness and the ability to be present in the moment: look past them to God.
We think of things we have to do, remember conversations, imagine scenarios. But as long as they come and go quickly and freely, we are still, at the same time, able to maintain attentiveness towards God.

These kinds of thoughts are light and do not attach themselves to passion or habitual patterns of thought. They just come and go, maintaining a kind of transparency. We remember little details of life, we think of things we should remember to do, we imagine things in the future. Our neurology just fires away, throwing little scenes up on the screen of consciousness. When these thoughts are light and transparent, we can almost see through them without having our conscious minds completely captured by them. Just as we are able to focus on our own conversation with a friend at a restaurant even when there is background conversation all around us, we can also continue in our loving worship of God even when light, transparent thoughts come and go.

Sometimes other more compelling or passionate thoughts momentarily capture the attention, closing down the open awareness to a narrow focus: notice the thought, name it and then return to the use of your word or phrase.
Worry, fear, anger, control, desire, and other gripping thoughts and emotions arise. Step out of them and notice what they are and the energy they carry, and name them before God, without analysis or interpretation. Then return to empty, expectant openness using your word or phrase.

Some thoughts or emotional activities are not light and transparent. They grab our attention, taking us far afield, and then later we wake up from their grip, wondering how we ever got there. What can help at this point is to name where we have been, without analysis: "obsessing about tonight's party...straining to figure out a problem... worrying about Mary...planning my day...trying to control my future...entertaining myself with images...."

The effect of this is that by naming our thoughts, we take away their power, because we temporarily step out of their grip, into a more objective place. The problem is, most of the time we believe our thoughts; we are caught up in them as if they are real. But they are not real. They are just neurological energy blips that habitually arise out of memory and learned experience.

To name gripping, involuntary thoughts specifically without analysis or judgment is to simply admit, before God, who we actually are in this moment, rather than who we think we are, or who we imagine ourselves to be. When we say, for the thousandth time, "trying to figure it all out...wondering how I can get things to go my way...escaping through fantasy..." we unmask the unconscious at work.

Instead of doing so with shame, we simply admit the truth of this moment before God. This is a gentle form of judgment, when we are caught with our pants down. We should be light about this, and if we are not, then we give ourselves another opportunity to name the ensuing self-judgment: "feeling terrible about my prayer...feeling I ought to be holier than I am...imagining God is disappointed with me...."

Many, though certainly not all, forms of meditation and contemplative prayer, including centering prayer, recommend that when one notices that any thought is arising in the silence, to quickly "let go" of the thought and return to the intention of prayer. While there is some benefit to this practice, I do not recommend it exclusively for the long haul. It is far too limited. It leaves out self-awareness, and its argument for doing so is that the self we are noticing in distractions is false. The more attention we give it, the more we believe it is real, and so the best thing to do is ignore it and instead, develop the real self, which is our capacity for empty, open, presence in God.

But this argument assumes that in paying attention to the false self, we are automatically caught up in it. It suggests that only two possibilities exist: either we are carried along unconsciously by habitual, ego-driven, mental activity, or we ignore it. There is a third possibility, and that is the process of seeing what our mind is doing without believing it. It is possible to notice, with great attention, what our mind is up to without being carried along by its passions.

I do not suggest that you stew over your thoughts in prayer, try to figure yourself out, allow your mind to take your consciousness where it wants to go, or think about thinking. I am not advocating that you obsess about what your mind is up to; I encourage you instead to lightly notice what it is doing. I am simply suggesting a way of coming to full conscious awareness about what the mind is up to, stepping outside the thought, noticing its intrigues and its passions, and holding that, too, before God as an honest self-offering of who you are in the moment. There is a big difference between being caught up in thinking and watching the mind. One is daydreaming, the other is awareness.

Let us say that when you sit in silence you tend to think of situations where you "failed" or did something "wrong," you beat yourself up about it mentally, and then try to imagine all the ways in which you could have done it "better." When you are caught up in thinking about this (daydreaming) you will just let this process play itself out, thereby, in fact, strengthening the sense that all of this is real, reinforcing a pattern of belief about yourself.

To notice that this is what you are doing is a far different matter. The consciousness comes to awareness either at the moment of thinking about something you have done "wrong," or it does so as you are in the middle of berating yourself or thinking of a better solution. At any point, you can step outside the pattern of thought and notice what the mind is doing, which is familiar to you because you have noticed it so many times before. In the noticing, naming, and feeling the energy that drives all this (self-condemnation, anger, fear, tightness in the body), you have effectively stopped the daydream and stood naked before God, holding the painful reality of your pattern as an honest self-offering. Usually at this point the thought pattern stops, and you can return to an empty, open awareness of prayer.

This contemplative prayer of self-awareness is not new to Christian spirituality. It is not "new age" or even psychologically modern in its development. In fact, the oldest and most continuously-practiced Christian tradition of contemplative prayer, the Eastern Orthodox prayer of the heart, specifically teaches as an essential part of prayer the practice of "watching the mind," or *nepsis*, as it is called in Greek. This is a practice of paying close attention to the kind of gripping thoughts that arise involuntarily during the silence, naming them for what they are, and thereby taking away their power. While the practitioners of this technique believed that demons are the source of gripping and passionate thoughts, they nevertheless showed a very sophisticated psychological awareness in the practice itself. *Nepsis* is a practice of intense, attentive self-awareness, combined with an open heart towards God.

The relationship between *nepsis* and the prayer of the heart is one that is summed up in this succinct, oft-repeated phrase: guarding the heart by watching the mind. In watching what the mind is up to, by naming it and holding it in honesty before God, we protect the open, vulnerable, loving place of precious encounter with God in the heart. We protect this precious place by *watching* the mind, because the incessant, controlling working of the mind is precisely what keeps us from staying connected with God in love and trust. It is as if, in prayer, we stand protectively over a vulnerable child, ready to confront any intruder who might come to disturb the safety of the child, quickly and accurately discerning the exact nature of the intruder's business.

The other reason this practice of watching the mind is so important is that if we never stop and pay attention to the content of involuntary thought, we will never come to understand over time the patterns of thought that are thrown up out of the unconscious, as visible manifestations of what is really going on down deep. It is as if the unconscious is trying to bring what is hidden to light by showing us, by means of our involuntary thoughts and "distractions," the precise nature of our deepest fantasies, fears, ambitions, cravings, our craziness, our desperate attempts to control. These are the very things that keep us separated from God, which Merton referred to as "the main obstacles keeping us from becoming [people] of prayer."

Whatever is going on in our little minds in the silence, it is best to come to reality about it. I do not think it is enough to simply shake our heads, amazed at and frustrated by the persistence of our distraction. immediately cast off any thought that arises, and re-commit to prayer. Instead, we can use what arises, especially habitually, as an opportunity to deepen our self-awareness, admitting who we are, and holding this judgment of truth before the God who knows it all already. This is part of the healing process of prayer.

After naming our thoughts, we then return to the open, empty awareness of an open-hearted presence before God, using the word or phrase we have selected, if helpful.

Sometimes an emotionally and physically charged or obsessive thought persists: simply feel its energy physically, stay with it as long as it lasts, and make this awareness your prayer.
Our attachments, fears, and ambitions not only grip us; they sometimes won't let go even when we name them and try to return to prayer via our word or phrase. In this case, drop your awareness below the content of the thought to the physical feeling that accompanies it: usually a contraction or tightness somewhere in the body. Just feel it for as long as it lasts. It will eventually pass. This self-offering is your prayer.

Here is where the practice becomes difficult. It is simple enough to label thoughts and emotions. But what if they persist, and you are really caught up in them? What you would like to do is get rid of them, re-commit to concentration on something "positive" and "spiritual," or just admit your inability to pray and get up and stop this nonsense. Instead, I suggest that you go deeper into what is pressing itself upon you. In order to do this, we must move beneath the thoughts themselves to the actual experience of what is driving them.

What I mean by this is that you drop below the thoughts into the body. There are always physical feelings that accompany the more persistent, gripping thoughts and emotions. The body does not lie. It knows what is going on. And the body tells you something that is true, something simpler and more concrete than anything words, ideas, or analysis can express.

And so I recommend that at this point you move your awareness into your body. When persistent thoughts or emotions remain, capturing your attention, and you have already labeled what you are doing, it is time to drop below to a deeper level. Place your awareness in your body. There will be some area of tightness, or a fluttery feeling, or some other sensation in your head, your chest, stomach, shoulders, or intestines. Remain in awareness of this sensation, not trying to change it or understand it. Be it.

In this way your thoughts will normally cease. What will remain is the actual experience of what is driving the thoughts. The engine that keeps the persistent distracting thoughts or emotions moving around will be revealed. You will be standing in its presence, feeling its energy. It is important to stress that this kind of attention is not a self-absorbed brooding over things that obsess us. That would only be more of the same old story: being caught up in the illusory creations of the false self. It is a clear, objective experiencing of strong patterns of thought and emotion in a physical way.

Even though this might feel scary or quite vulnerable, it is a simple place, really, and awareness can be very clear here. It can actually be a relief to drop down into this place of pure fear, or control, or anger, or confusion. It has a purity. It just is what it is. Again, this is a place of real truth, where we stand under the loving light of God's judgment, exposed for who we are at our deepest core. It is holy ground.

At this point, simply to stand on this holy ground is our prayer. For there is no better form of prayer than to be who we are in the presence of God. We remain here as long as we need to. Eventually the physical sensation will pass, and peace will come.

Close the time of contemplation with a prayer of thanksgiving and dedication.

Your time of prayer may have been dominated by simple, open awareness and worship; by light, transparent thoughts; by heartfelt devotion to God; by occasional gripping thoughts interspersed with worship; or by the experience of dropping below thought to physical sensations of something quite unsettling.

In any case, it is all held in God's grace. Whatever has or has not taken place, we need not worry about its effectiveness. We only pray that God will use our time to bring us more fully into eternal life. Keep in mind that prayer is God's work in us far more than it is our work. Prayer requires our effort, to be sure, but God is at work even when we think we have failed at prayer. Contemplative prayer requires faith, faith in God's activity of grace within, undertaken in response to our invitation and genuine desire.

In Summary

Again, we must balance flexibility and commitment in prayer, moving with the Spirit and also being willing to go deeply into a practice that can only bear fruit over time. While you may not need to include all the elements of this approach to prayer every time you pray, over the years you may find that each of its components has its place in your prayer life. There is something important, over the years, about each piece: we must learn to become grounded in our body when we pray, dependent upon God's grace even in order to be able to pray, tender-hearted and vulnerable, focused through an open and non-manipulative intention, and honest and humble about ourselves as the false self rises to consciousness.

It may be useful, if one is beginning, to first focus on the elemental act of just sitting still in silence and feeling one's breath, in the presence of God. This takes some getting used to. Beginners usually have to struggle with an avalanche of thoughts as they first enter into silence; in this case, the frequent use of a word or phrase, even repeated constantly like a mantra, may be exactly what you need to do in order to create a little open space mentally.

If this initial work is not so necessary, then remain with whatever portion of this approach that seems the right place to be. If you have already done a lot of work that has enabled you to know how to be present in the moment, to gripping thoughts and the emotional drama that arises out of your brokenness, you may not need to practice it in your prayer life as much as others do. In this case, you might be called to simply hold your loving desire for God with an open heart. Alternatively, you may be going through a particularly difficult phase where you cannot do anything but pay attention to insistent and intense emotions and thoughts that arise.

In order to discern what we need at any given time in prayer, all of us need help from more experienced people. Certainly the Spirit will guide us in prayer, but one of the ways the Spirit does so is through a spiritual director. To undertake a serious and sustained practice of contemplative prayer, it is essential to be in regular conversation with someone who is able to assist in the discernment process. If a spiritual director who is experienced in contemplative prayer is not immediately available to you in your area, you might consider a telephone or e-mail relationship. In any case, it is difficult to see ourselves, and we all need the eyes and advice of another when it comes to our movement into the life of faith.

Finally, let me offer some advice about developing a habit of prayer. Many, but not all, find that arising a little earlier in the morning allows one to approach prayer with a freshness that the middle or end of the day cannot provide. The loss of sleep is usually recovered through the prayer itself, as the stillness of contemplation gives a different kind of rest to the body. Do not expect to be able to plunge immediately into a daily practice. Begin as often as you can, without berating yourself for the times you do not get up to pray. Soon the benefit of prayer will motivate you to do it, so that it moves from being a discipline to something that you enjoy and look forward to. Remember that prayer is a relationship, not a job, and relationships take time to develop and give evidence of their fruits.

Begin with a few minutes of silence, perhaps ten to fifteen. Over time you will naturally want to expand this time, moving eventually to a half hour or more. Length of time is less important than the quality of time spent. Some find that two or three fifteen minute meditations in the day work better than one longer one.

I also recommend that you create a small, simple altar space in your home that you use habitually for prayer. There is something about us humans that responds well to a sense of place. Our bodies, senses, mind, and heart are all intertwined, and having an external place of prayer can help us to find the internal place of prayer as well. We learn to associate the habit of place with the habit of mind and heart. A box or low table, a candle, perhaps a print of an icon or a flower, some incense: after awhile these sensory objects serve as a kind of spiritual magnet, pulling us into the interior state of prayer.

Gradually our efforts, our habits of discipline and specific practices open us up to something that is quite beyond all these human details. At some point we become aware of the fact that in prayer we have moved into a holy mystery, which is the very life of God in and around us. In this mystery, in this relationship of love, we do our part to remain present to both God and ourselves, and God, in turn, slowly affects a transformation of our very being. This transformation eventually makes us truer to who we really are, truer to the kingdom of heaven, truer to Christ, in whose image we are all made.

Two

❀

Praying with the Will, the Mind, and the Heart

M OST OF US WHO SERIOUSLY PURSUE a spiritual path eventually learn that the journey we have undertaken must encompass all of our lives. Over time, nothing is left out. We must bring into our faith the relationships we live with, our work, the world we inhabit, our beliefs about life, our heart-felt longings for God, our emotions and personal struggles, our physical health, and everything else. When any one of these dimensions of our lives suffers, our whole being is affected. Spirituality cannot be cordoned off as one discreet dimension, having only to do with the "soul," as if our lives were like a popular magazine, with a spirituality section distinct from those that have to do with politics, economy, health, and human interest.

One common and useful way of seeing the holistic nature of life in God is to invoke the familiar balance of body, mind, and spirit. Our physicality, our mental-emotional states and our spirituality are inseparable, completely intertwined. Jesus himself recognized this when he reminded us of the first commandment, to "love the Lord your God with all your heart, and with all your soul, and with all your mind, and with all your strength" (Mark 12:30). We must learn to love the Lord in ways that employ all our God-given capacities: emotion, intellect, will, activity, and soul. In the most influential spiritual tradition of the Christian West, monasticism, this holistic approach to life in God includes the practices of prayer, study, and work (in another book, I explore these traditional Benedictine disciplines).[1]

But the holistic claim of God on our lives has to do not only with these large dimensions of our being and activity. Wholeness must also extend into the ways we pray, too. Every historic religion tradition of prayer and meditation has methods of doing this. Buddhists, Hindus, Muslims, Jews and Christians all have ways of praying that include body (bowing, incense, chanting, sitting, and breathing). All include the mind (study and reflection, watching the mind). All involve the heart (devotion, opening the heart, surrender, and letting-go into God).

In this chapter I would like to go deeper, beyond the rudimentary instructions of the first chapter, into a holistic way of praying contemplatively. I offer this three-dimensional model in order not only to present the wholeness of prayer, but also to address the differing needs of a diversity of people. At varying times, each of us might be better served by an approach to prayer that emphasizes either the heart, the soul, the mind, or our strength. In any given period of prayer, it is also possible to flow from one of these dimensions to the next.

One way of seeing how we can pray with heart, soul, mind, and strength is through the traditional model of the individual's journey of faith that has been taught throughout Christendom, East and West, especially in the middle ages. This model sees the journey as including purification, illumination, and union with God. Purification can be seen as the approach to God that includes strength, the body, effort, and the will. Illumination involves the mind, and union, the heart.

---

1 Brian Taylor, *Spirituality for Everyday Living: an Adaptation of the Rule of St. Benedict* (Collegeville: Liturgical Press, 1989).

Many of the medieval authors on the subject tended to see this schema as a kind of ladder, suggesting that the rank beginner must first focus solely on purification: repentance, change of behavior, the use of the will and determination in order to turn to a more holy life. For these authors, purification is the process of moral conversion, which starts when one stops sinful behaviors and begins pious ones. The intermediate, having mastered moral purification, then moves on to illumination: being guided by the Spirit into a greater understanding of the self and God. Illumination is the process of study and reflection whereby one develops faith and learns about what the Bible and the church's theology teaches. The advanced few then climb to the heights of contemplative union, leaving behind all else. Union is seen as the state of being completely under the influence of God's grace, whereby all separation between human and divine is overcome, and one receives the inflow of God's joy, peace, and other fruits of the Spirit.

There is some truth to this ladder-like view. It is hard to grow in our understanding of the faith if we have not yet put behind us behaviors that prevent such understanding. It is hard to find union with God unless we have done some conversion of life and also examined our faith. However, the medieval ladder approach as such is more hierarchical, systematized, and linear than the teaching of earlier writers who proposed it in the first place.

More ancient Christian mystics understood that every Christian has to continually employ the will and effort, since the process of spiritual purification goes on through all of life; every Christian must always seek spiritual illumination through understanding and learning; and every Christian has access to conscious union with God, at least from time to time, no matter how "rudimentary" or "advanced" we are spiritually. They are really just three overlapping dimensions of our relationship with God, rather than three distinct stages we must pass through. While one of these practices may need to be more dominant in our lives at times than others, we will always need to attend to all three.

And so if we look at purification, illumination, and union in this way, we can see that this model proposes not only a ladder of perfection, but also a way of entering into relationship with God through various means, each of which is called for at various times.

Traditionally, in this three-fold schema, purification has usually addressed that part of our faith life that has to do with moral behavior, the avoidance of sin, and the practice of virtue. Illumination has to do with study and learning, and union with contemplative prayer. However, for the purposes of this chapter, which concerns itself with the development of a practice of contemplative prayer, I will confine my discussion of these three dimensions to the ways in which they relate specifically to contemplative prayer.

Purification can be practiced in contemplative prayer through our wills and efforts. To begin with, we must get up in the morning, we must try, we must work at developing habits of contemplative prayer. We must also bring awareness through our bodies in a concentrated way, sitting still, keeping our consciousness fixed on our breath, our senses, on a word or phrase. By employing our wills, we bring attention to our practice. The Buddhist training in mindfulness is a good example of this part of prayer. Our lives become more purified through this attentive effort in prayer.

Illumination comes as we learn about ourselves in the silence of contemplation. We watch our mind and emotions at work in the form of involuntary thought and emotional activity (commonly called "distractions"). By doing so we come to understand more about ourselves as we really are; we grow in self-awareness. Prayer developed by Ignatius of Loyola and his religious order, the Jesuits, is an example of this kind of prayer, which examines both the conscience and what comes up in the imagination. Our lives become more illumined through this process of prayerful self-awareness.

Union is the underlying reality of life in God, of which we seek to be conscious in contemplative prayer. Specific practices for this include surrender, not being effortful or self-aware, letting go of all thoughts, and sitting in silent, loving devotion to the One who is all in all. We open the heart to that which already is: our union with God. Centering prayer focuses on this particular dimension of contemplation. We see our unity with God more and more, through this prayer of opening and surrender.

Here, then, is the way in which I will be approaching a holistic contemplative practice. Loving God with our strength includes effort and will, physical dedication, attention, and concentration, and this leads to a kind of purification, simplification, and clarification of our lives. Loving God with our mind and heart includes watching involuntary thoughts and emotions in the silence, coming to illumination through self-awareness. Loving God with our soul includes opening the heart and surrender, which leads to an experience of our union with the divine.

My own orientation to contemplative prayer is through the Eastern Christian prayer of the heart. This kind of prayer is also known through one of its forms, the Jesus Prayer, or by the Greek word for "stillness," *hesychasm*. While its name "prayer of the heart" seems to emphasize only the third dimension of prayer (union) that has to do with surrender and opening the heart, it actually encompasses concentration (purification) and self-awareness (illumination) as well.

I will say much more about this in the next chapter, but for now it might be helpful to know that in this most ancient and continuous of Christian contemplative traditions, all three dimensions I address here come together: the will, the mind, and the heart (attention, awareness, and opening to God). It is for this reason that many of my examples and quotations come from this tradition. But in using these examples, I do not mean to imply that this holism is absent from other Christian contemplative paths. The same patterns can be seen throughout the wide diversity of our rich history of spirituality and mysticism. It is just that for me, the clarity of this three-fold inter-relationship is more evident in the prayer of the heart.

Again, it may be that right now, one of these three dimensions of prayer will speak to you more than the other two. It may be that your personality is generally more oriented to one than the other. But as every religious tradition teaches, we are called to broaden our practice of prayer and meditation so that it utilizes, eventually, our whole being: the will, the mind, and the heart. We can do this through praying with concentration, self-awareness, and opening to God. By the grace of God, we are led through these means to greater purification, illumination, and union.

Praying with the Will: Purification

As I begin this discussion, I must make it clear that when I speak of employing the will in prayer, I am not suggesting a kind of willful, self-sufficient, macho approach to prayer. All prayer must have an openness to the Spirit, a reliance upon God to accomplish in us what we ultimately cannot do. We are incapable of clawing our way, by sheer will power, into the peace of God.

And yet, it is true that without effort, we will not get anywhere in prayer. We must develop the habit of setting aside a daily time for prayer, turn from activities that separate us from God, and try to be present in contemplation. Then God begins to move in response to our intention and desire. So there is a relationship between our effort and the beginnings of the movement of grace in our lives. It is almost as if our efforts prime the pump so that the grace of God can begin flowing. The twelfth century Peter of Damaskos quotes John Chrysostom in speaking of this relationship of effort and grace:

> Human effort is profitless without help from above; but no one receives such help unless he himself chooses to make an effort, says St. John Chrysostom.[2]

The Syrian desert father known as Pseudo-Macarius (called pseudo because he wrote or was remembered in the name of the earlier Egyptian, Macarius the Great, perhaps to honor him) in describing the first steps that are necessary in the life of holiness, also speaks of effort as a kind of foundation:

> There is need of much labor and sweat so as to seek and lay down a foundation…in this way we begin to grow in sanctity. (Homily 15.53)[3]

This foundation that is laid in contemplative prayer can come through the practice of concentration. By bringing the effort of attention to bear on our prayer, it helps us focus, slow down, inhabit our bodies in the here and now, and be present to God. What might this practice of contemplative concentration look like?

As I outlined in the first chapter, it begins with attention to the body. By sitting up straight, we are not only able to stay still for longer periods of time; we also, through physical attentiveness, bring clarity to the mind. A body that is alert, relaxed, and still will affect mental and spiritual alertness, relaxation, and stillness.

---

2 *The Philokalia, Vol. III* (London: Faber and Faber, 1984), 167.
3 *Pseudo-Macarius: the 50 Spiritual Homilies and the Great Letter*, trans. George A. Maloney, SJ (New York: Paulist Press, 1992), 128.

As we begin our time of prayer, it helps to focus first on the breath. Knowing that God is intimately present, even in our bodies, we feel the divine breath of life as it flows in and out. Feeling our bodies, the air around our skin, the gentle force of gravity; hearing and seeing all that is around us like a beautiful landscape of this moment; we begin to slow down, to be here and now. This may sound gentle and easy as I describe it, but sometimes it takes real effort to stay present with the physical. We must be determined to bring our minds back to this grounding reality every time it strays. We must use our wills to be present.

After some minutes of this physical awakening, our concentration can then move to our intentions for prayer. Through the use of a word or phrase that is repeated constantly or occasionally, we keep the mind on a short leash. As it wanders, we bring it back to this moment in God, saying something like "opening to you," "Lord Jesus have mercy," "help me to pray," "thank you,"or "here I am." Focus on the words, and on the intention behind the words. Let your desire for God be encapsulated in these words. Unite your saying of the word or phrase to your breath, so that body and mind are one.

In the use of the Jesus Prayer, the ancient teachers recommend that we concentrate our minds on the words themselves: "Lord Jesus Christ, have mercy on me." Rather than focusing in a way that seeks to understand the meaning of this phrase, as if we were exploring it mentally and imaginatively, we are advised to penetrate its intention. Fully desiring God's loving mercy, we keep saying this phrase with complete attention, invoking what we desire with real intensity. When the mind is firmly fixed on this phrase, the teachers say, all other thoughts are pushed out, and the heart is opened to God. The fourteenth century Nicephorus the Solitary advised:

Force [the mind], instead of all other thought, to have only this one constant cry within. If you continue to do this constantly, with your whole attention, then in time this will open for you the way to the heart.[4]

This intensity of desire is an expression of our will. It takes concentration, or as Macarius says, "labor and sweat." It is probably best done with a mantra, like the Jesus Prayer, said over and over with the breath. The contemplative teacher and author John Main has written much on this subject. Contrary to some popular belief (perhaps evoked by stereotypes of dancing, tambourine-beating, orange-clad people blissfully chanting *Hare Krishna*), the purpose of a mantra is not to get oneself into a trance-like altered state. It is a way of completely focusing the attention, fully awake in this moment, towards God. As the nineteenth century Russian Bishop Ignatii said:

The essential, indispensable element in prayer is attention. Without attention there is no prayer.[5]

Alternatively, many find that words are not helpful in terms of focusing the mind towards God. Feeling the breath can be enough, following it through the nostrils, into the body and out again. But whether words or the breath are used, the work and its effect are the same. Having centered ourselves in the body and through our senses, having focused our wills and desires towards God, our thoughts do slow down. It becomes clear that we are not just sitting in silence in order to daydream; we are in the presence of the Holy One. In light of this presence, the message we are giving to ourselves through

---

4 *Writings from the Philokalia on Prayer of the Heart*, trans.
E. Kadloubovsky and G.E.H. Palmer (London: Faber and Faber, 1951), 34.
5 *The Art of Prayer*, 104.

concentration is "Wake up!" Focusing our attention through breath, body, senses, intention, and desire, we hold ourselves before God as a self-offering.

Through the use of our wills in prayer, a kind of purification takes place. As our intention and desires for God become more strongly felt and expressed, we are actually in the process of turning our lives towards God. This is, after all, what "repentance" means: to turn. Through concentration, we turn away from all that would distract and hinder us from God, and we turn towards the very Source of our lives.

Sometimes this kind of concentrated prayer is all we can do. By pushing out all other thoughts and forcing the mind to stay in one place, it is the only thing that allows us to be present and awake. Other times it will not work at all. Other thoughts are just too persistent. It is also possible that in the normal course of our times of prayer, we can always begin with this attentive concentration as a way of starting prayer, slowing down, clarifying our intent, and readying ourselves for what might come next. And what comes next, usually, is what we often call "distractions:" involuntary, seemingly random thoughts and emotional activity. So we must learn to pray with our minds, moving into self-awareness.

Praying with the Mind: Illumination

In our intention to be present to God in prayer, we use a word or a phrase or the breath to keep ourselves focused. But even as we do this, the mind will want to wander around as it usually does throughout our day. In fact, we cannot prevent this wandering. No matter how much will power and concentration we try to use, we cannot make ourselves stay undistracted in prayer. The mind has a mind of its own. It grasps on insistently to memories, problems, fantasies; it scrutinizes, worries, and plans.

If we pay attention to the kinds of thoughts and emotional activity that are repeated over and over, we notice that our minds tend to generate the same types continually. We may discover that our minds are frequently engaged in efforts to control the future by planning everything out. The mind could be feeling angry about ourselves or others, casting about for blame. It may be working hard to understand all the events and relationships of our lives. It might manufacture elaborate fantasies, almost like little movies that put us in imagined sexual encounters, dangerous circumstances, and exotic locations.

But why should we want to pay attention to all this? Many teachers of prayer and meditation call this seemingly random mental and emotional activity "monkey mind," a meaningless, random expression of the ego; and they point out the danger that by paying attention to it, we only give it more power. The solution, they say, is not to employ the mind to try to tame the mind. A vivid image that some teachers use is the man who walks on a plank, trying to remove the plank even as he walks on it. To use the mind to understand or control the mind is impossible, and the effort to do so only complicates matters. The solution instead is to short-circuit the mind entirely, by ignoring it, focusing instead on God.

There is some truth to this. If all we are doing in prayer is getting caught up in our mental and emotional distractions, we are doing nothing different than what we tend to do all day long in our daydreaming. And if we spend our time in prayer by trying to control or understand our thoughts, the situation becomes even worse: at this point, we are even more caught up in the workings of monkey mind.

This advice has great merit, and there are times when it must be followed, when we are better off not paying attention to what the mind is doing. Beginners, especially, should probably heed this particular caution. They might profit more by practicing the kind of concentrated meditation that I cover in the previous section of this chapter (or a heart-centered prayer, which I cover in the next), learning to screen out, let go of, or quiet down all thoughts, just so that they can learn how to be still and present to God.

However, it is possible to bring an awareness to our "distractions" in prayer in a way that is quite different from being caught up in them. We can learn to take a small step out of the thoughts even as they are in the process of taking place, notice what they are, feel their energy, name them before God, and then return to the stillness of the contemplative moment at hand. In Buddhist meditation, this is referred to as becoming the observer rather than the subject of what is going on. To be the observer simply means that we notice, feel, name, and offer what is emerging mentally and emotionally in the silence. We do this without interpretation, control, elaboration, condemnation, or praise. We simply see what is there.

When we do this, we notice that many of our thoughts are about the past and the future. We obsess over what we have done or have not done, what could happen or what we are afraid might happen. We spin off into fantasies, often discovering we have done so only after several minutes have gone by. Where have we been? Certainly not here and now. Becoming the observer, we simply begin to notice exactly what we're doing.

But again, why do this? Because, I believe, part of the purpose and effect of contemplative prayer and meditation is the healing of our brokenness. This brokenness—our anger, fear, control, self-condemnation, and guilt-always emerges in the silence. If we watch our thoughts, we will see it all. We see how the mind worries or blames, and how the body tenses up when it does so. We see how it avoids pain by taking us away into entertaining imagination. We see just how determined we are to get our way as we watch the mind planning everything out. Healing in contemplation is possible when in the emptiness of silent prayer, the brokenness of our lives is allowed to come to the surface, where we can see it and God can touch it.

The danger in not observing our minds and emotions in some way or another (and there are other ways of coming to self-awareness, to be sure) is that in spite of our skill in contemplation, there will have been no healing. When this happens, we have built up a spiritual identity that is pious and peaceful, or willfully focused, on top of a very shaky foundation. Without the healing that comes through honest, humble self-awareness, we might learn how to be still, but underneath the stillness is all the same old control, fear, anger, or escapism, ready to emerge again in our lives as soon as we get up from the cushion.

This may sound terribly pessimistic, as if everything about us below the conscious level is bad, twisted, and dark, just waiting to pop up in the silence. It is certainly true that there is much that is good about us: we love, we want to be present to God, we have good intentions. But our goodness does not really need awareness. It just is, and we can give thanks to God for it. What needs self-awareness is the brokenness that needs healing.

While all of us have been gifted with many wonderful qualities, all of us also were born into an imperfect world and were affected by difficult circumstances. We developed ways of coping with this imperfection and difficulty that work to some degree, but eventually these same coping mechanisms turn against us and become destructive. They become an unintentional way of separating ourselves from others, from happiness and freedom, from God. Our abilities to problem solve and take care of ourselves turn into control. Our capacities for love and empathy turn into self-neglect and the desire to please everyone. Our strength to stand up for ourselves and not tolerate wrong-doing becomes blame and self-righteousness.

As we sit in silence, these behaviors will reveal themselves in the form of mental and emotional patterns. As we observe the involuntary thoughts and emotions that arise in silence, we see ourselves, again and again, trying to control, condemn, please, understand, or justify. Contemplation includes not only worship; it also involves the painful process of coming to self-awareness of all that is broken in us, all that separates us from God. Prayer involves the recognition of what we do to prevent prayer.

Without a clear understanding of exactly how habitual patterns of the mind and emotions encumber us, we cannot attain simplicity of spirit; the Spirit has no space, no freedom to move. An anonymous Greek monk of Mount Athos had this to say about self-awareness:

> The primordial condition [to prayer] and absolute necessity is to know oneself. To gain this knowledge the beginner must learn to be alive to the many-sided possibilities of the ego; and he must eliminate all obstacles, personal as well as external, to acquire the best conditions for success.[6]

This self-awareness is a kind of illumination, given to us by the Spirit within. In this sense, we can see that perhaps the "observer" is nothing less than the point of view of the Holy Spirit, showing us the truth about ourselves. As Jesus said, the Holy Spirit "will guide you into all the truth" (John 16:13), and "you will know the truth, and the truth will make you free" (John 8:32). As the Spirit brings us to self-awareness, as God illumines what is otherwise kept in the dark of our unconscious

---

6 *Writings from the Philokalia on Prayer of the Heart*, 5.

mind, what is illumined is eventually healed. Just as a plant that is unhealthy must sometimes be exposed to the light, so must our unconscious minds reveal themselves, be observed, named, known, and held before God in the light of awareness.

This, I believe, is the real function of God's judgment. Many of us these days tend to associate this word with judgmentalism, but they are not the same thing. Think of a loving mother, who calls her child to accountability and speaks the truth to him about his behavior, and does so without ever compromising the love she has for the child. This is loving judgment.

God's judgment is the truth about ourselves, brought into the light, even as we are held in the hands of God in complete, unconditional, forgiving love. We are held accountable in the truth of loving judgment, but we are never condemned. Sitting in silence, watching the mind, being the observer, seeing ourselves as we really are, rather than as we wish we could be: this is the loving judgment of God, the illumination of the Holy Spirit, leading us into all truth.

Healing comes as we face the truth about ourselves, as we see and feel just what our brokenness is exactly about. Feeling the physical tension, noticing the quality of the mind's activity, holding it before God as an honest, humble, self-offering, healing comes. By bringing awareness to the ways in which we keep ourselves distracted or in control, we place them before God's feet. Instead of being caught up in our patterns of mental and emotional activity, instead of ignoring them altogether, we come to honest self-awareness and hold ourselves, as we are, before the One who will take us as we are and heal us.

A teacher of mine for many years, Joko Beck, is one of those contemporary teachers of meditation who recommends bringing awareness to the content of seemingly random thoughts, knowing, as she does, that the effect of this practice is profoundly healing. She says:

> When we practice like this, we get acquainted with ourselves, how our lives work, what we are doing with them...When we label thoughts precisely and carefully, what happens to them? They begin to quiet down. We don't have to force ourselves to get rid of them...we don't just do this three times, we do it ten thousand times; and as we do it, our life transforms.[7]

I am not suggesting that during contemplative prayer we interpret our thinking, wondering about why we think and feel what we do. Instead, I recommend that in prayer, we simply notice what the mind is up to, step a little bit aside, feel the energy of the thought or emotion, name it before God objectively, and without interpretation or explanation, offer this humbly and honestly to God, and then return to the silence and stillness of the moment.

The process of naming and offering I suggest here is quite simple. When you notice that you are already in the middle of a thought, take a step outside it, and say silently to God precisely what it is that you are doing. You might say something like one of the following: "planning everything out...regretting something I said...trying to understand someone... judging myself...judging others...imagining disaster... imagining success...feeling angry at her...feeling afraid." Then drop your awareness into the body, feeling the energy of the thought. Feel the quality of energy, the location of the tension or light-headedness or fluttery chest. Hold this quality in your awareness before God as an offering of who you are in this moment.

---

7 Charlotte Joko Beck, *Everyday Zen* (San Francisco: Harper and Row, 1989) 27.

Since our normal way of operating is to try to control the process, awareness usually leads us into an attempt to change ourselves. Perhaps we notice what we are doing in our thinking and we immediately tell God what to do about it: "Here I am again, Lord, worrying...I shouldn't worry...please remove my fear." This can be just another method of trying to judge and control our reality.

What I am suggesting instead is a radically different approach that is rooted in naked faith. We simply notice, name, feel, and hold before God our conditioned and habitual reactivity, our fears and attachments and attempts to control. We do not go the next step into trying to figure it out, change it, or even ask for it to be removed from us. Instead, we simply open ourselves up to God as we are, full of empty and expectant awareness, feeling what we are feeling, trusting that the divine light will slowly do whatever is necessary to heal us over time.

As indicated by the quotation above from the anonymous monk of Mt. Athos, the practice of self-awareness is very much a part of contemplation in the Eastern prayer of the heart/Jesus Prayer. For the early desert and Orthodox monks, persistent and distracting thoughts in prayer were originally seen as demons, and still, by some. One might be troubled continually by the demon of anger, or greed, envy, or lust. While they didn't think in modern psychological terms, they certainly understood what we now call psychological obstacles. They called them demons, and knew that sometimes they not only needed to be cast out or ignored; they also needed to be exposed and named quite specifically. By naming the demon, one gained some power over it.

One of the earliest of the desert fathers, fourth century Evagrius Ponticus, was particularly insightful about this, advising (as does Joko Beck, above) the contemplative monk to precisely and accurately name their personal demons, to:

....address effective words against them, that is
to say, those words which correctly characterize
the one present. And we must do this before
they drive us out of our own state of mind.[8]

In this early desert tradition that continues to this day
through Orthodox monastic life, this practice of
watching one's thoughts is called *nepsis*. *Nepsis* has to do
with a careful observation of the kinds of thoughts that
arise in the silence, not being swept along by thoughts
or analyzing them, but noting the character or quality of
them. Again, an insight from Evagrius:

....let him keep careful watch over his thoughts.
Let him observe their intensity, their periods of
decline and follow them as they rise and fall.
Let him note well the complexity of his thoughts,
their periodicity, the demons which cause them,
with the order of their succession and the nature
of their associations.[9]

And so here in the fourth century, we have the
beginnings of an almost psychological approach to
contemplative prayer. Evagrius, and every teacher of this
tradition after him, teaches the contemplative to be an
observer of the mind as it reveals itself in the silence.
While in our day, we may not identify the source of
mental/emotional patterns of attachment, fear, anger, or
control as demonic or evil, we can appreciate the
practice of *nepsis* nonetheless. Another term that the
eastern contemplatives use for this same practice is
guarding the heart by watching the mind. This is a
particularly poignant way of putting it.

Through *nepsis*, we try to guard the heart by keeping
watch over the mind, by seeing what it is up to. In so

---

8 Evagrius Ponticus, *The Praktikos and Chapters on Prayer*
(Kalamazoo: Cistercian Publications, 1978), p. 28 (Praktikos 43).
9 Ibid, p.30 (Praktikos 50).

doing, we guard the simplicity, tenderness, and holiness of the heart-the place where the Spirit is encountered and worshiped-by paying attention to the kinds of things that would take us away from it. By attending to the particular ways in which we separate ourselves from union with God, we actually guard, or protect the ability of the heart to open up to the Spirit. To repeat the image of the first chapter: it is as if the mind, sharpened and attentive, stands guard over a tender child (the heart), ready to confront any intruder and discern the exact nature of his business there. Part of the task of prayer is to keep vigilance over the purity of the heart, to protect it against everything that would prevent its opening.

Without this protection, our hearts do not have a chance. They will forever be at the mercy of reactive thoughts, our personal demons, if you will, that distract our intentions to be open and vulnerable to God. When we come to self-knowledge, however, and name our habitual thoughts and emotions for what they are, we eventually "cast them out," thereby creating space for our hearts to be open and simple. At this point we are less dominated by them, and can worship freely. If we do this enough, we will weaken them considerably, and the familiar patterns of reactivity, control, and fear that arise out of our brokenness will have little power over us. We may never be rid of these patterns entirely, since they are a part of our unique, conditioned humanity, but at least we will be able to see them as they arise, and expose, and offer them to God before they take us wherever they want us to go. And that is a considerable amount of freedom, born out of the healing power of illumination.

Praying with the Heart: Union

To even speak about experiencing "union with God" is intimidating and potentially arrogant, idolatrous. This intimidation is partly rooted in medieval writings that tended to emphasize the higher degrees of unitive selflessness that are characterized by uninterrupted joy. I will be taking a broader, humbler approach when I speak of union. But the danger is also rooted in being too flip about what we call "union." God's being is, after all, transcendent to all our experience and understanding. So when we speak of contemplative union, we are really only describing that portion of the divine presence that we can sense, and which we can sense only because it is given as a gift to us by God.

As I described in the beginning of this book, most of us have experienced brief moments of peace, joy, selfless wonder, interconnectedness, and complete love. I do not make a distinction between these moments and some theoretical state of complete and permanent union with the divine. It's all on a continuum, with the distinguishing differences being perhaps depth, duration, or frequency of the experience. So as I speak of union in this section, I am coming from a belief that it is somewhat accessible for all who seek God. After all, why would God be available only to a few? Time, dedication, patience, faith, love for God, and grace are the factors that tend to make the difference between an occasional, random sense of union and one that is more familiar and frequent.

And yet, no amount of dedication or experience with prayer makes it possible to turn something that is essentially a gift into something we can control. Only God can give the gift of conscious, experiential awareness of God's holy presence. But we can learn how to open to this possibility, and to remove the obstacles that stand in its way. That is what this section is really about: opening to the possibility of the gift of contemplation. In this sense, everything that we do in terms of contemplative prayer is actually just preparation for contemplation itself, which is another word for the experience of God's gift of conscious union.

In this chapter we began by looking at ways in which we utilize our wills and our efforts in prayer. We called this purification, since it involves the purifying work of turning to God, its contemplative expression has to do with staying focused through the use of a mantra or other concentrative practice. We then examined the process of illumination, where through self-awareness, we pay attention to the mind and emotions as they reveal themselves in the form of "distractions." By this kind of awareness, we get to know ourselves, especially our brokenness, better.

In a sense, praying with the will and with self-awareness about the mind are about us more than they are about God. God, of course, is present in these forms of prayer, and we do aim our focused wills and our offerings of self-awareness towards God. But they're still part of the process of preparation for what comes next, which is not about us at all. It is about God. After all, prayer is not all about us, our needs, our efforts, our consciousness. Prayer, especially unitive, contemplative prayer, is also worship and adoration of the One who is the Source of all that is.

There is a time in our prayer to turn away from self-awareness, to transcend our problems and obstacles, and to simply empty ourselves and be open to the God who is. As important as it is to offer ourselves as we are to God, it is just as important to worship God for being God. It is to this worship that we now turn in the practice of "praying with the heart." For it is in the heart that we are able to be most open to God and to worship in a way that is self-emptying and self-transcending.

When I use this term, it may be helpful to remember that the Eastern Orthodox prayer of the heart is a general term that refers to contemplative prayer itself, and not just praying in a heart-centered way. The prayer of the heart is a broad practice that includes a utilization of the will and concentration through the Jesus Prayer mantra, the self-awareness of *nepsis* (watching the mind), and the heart-centered, self-emptying adoration of God. Again, it is both effort and self-awareness that prepare the way for the prayer of contemplative union in the heart.

In this section, then, I will be sharing that particular dimension of the Eastern contemplative prayer of the heart that deals specifically with the practice of praying with the heart. This dimension of the wonderfully rich contemplative tradition of the Christian East is perhaps most succinctly summarized by the nineteenth century Russian Bishop Theophan the Recluse in this way:

> With the mind firmly established in the heart,
> stand before the Lord with awe, reverence,
> and devotion.[10]

A heart-centered form of contemplative prayer, then, consists of the mind (or the consciousness) rooted in the heart, maintaining an attitude of loving reverence towards God. While one may continue to use the Jesus Prayer (or some other phrase or word) to keep centered, we drop our consciousness below the level of self-awareness, words, even the mantra, into the heart, where the Spirit is to be encountered. Leaving everything about ourselves behind, we keep the awareness at a deeper level of being. Again, Theophan says:

> In purely contemplative prayer, words and
> thoughts themselves disappear, not by our own
> wish, but of their own accord…it may consist
> only in a standing before God, in an opening of
> the heart to him in reverence and love.[11]

What does it mean to speak of "the mind in the heart?" How on earth do we do it? First of all, it should be understood here that in this tradition the "heart" is understood holistically: as the physical organ, as the

---

10 *The Art of Prayer*, 61.
11 Ibid., 72.

source of our emotional lives, and as the very center of our soul. Pseudo-Macarius was one of the clearest early voices expressing this holistic view of "the heart:"

> The heart directs and governs all the other organs of the body...There, in the heart, the mind abides as well as all the thoughts of the soul and all its hopes. (*Homily* 15.20)[12]

And so the "heart" is the center of our whole being: mind, body, soul, and spirit. In the prayer of the heart, our attention (or the mind) drops down out of our head and into the fullness of our being, into the heart. It is like moving out of a busy week when we've been terribly occupied with many things, climbing a large hill and just sitting up there, looking out over the horizon, feeling the breeze, letting go of everything but this moment. In the prayer of the heart, we stop being just our thoughts and our efforts to pray, and we become much more: our breath, light, sound, our bodies, and most importantly, God's loving presence.

To move the awareness from head to heart, it can be useful to focus the attention on the center of the chest, and imagine that the heart is opening, softening, warming, and becoming vulnerable to God. For some, this means an actual visualization of the heart itself, or following the breath down into the chest. Others simply place their attention in the center of their bodies. And so in this prayer we keep our awareness in the heart, in the very center of our body, which is the symbolic center of our being and the location of love, even to the point of feeling a warmth in the chest as we pray. This warmth, for the Orthodox, is a sign that one is connected to the Spirit, who lives within the heart.

In whatever way works for you, keep your attention on this place, feeling, if you can, the heart within the chest,

---

12 *Pseudo-Macarius*, 116.

and the rising and falling that comes with each breath. As your mind wanders, bring it back to this focus through the heart, the chest, the breath. Keep your mind's attention centered here. Maintain a sense of your love for God pouring out of your heart and God's love for you pouring into it.

This Orthodox practice of heart-meditation is remarkably close to other traditions from other places and times. In seventeenth century Europe, a devotion to the Sacred Heart of Jesus developed (and continues to this day), where the one who prays holds the image of Jesus' physical heart in mind, pouring out one's love to him, and also receiving his love. It is also similar to the *chakra* systems of both Hindu and Chinese Taoist meditation, whereby one opens the heart *chakra* in order to experience the energy (or *prana, chi*) of love that is present in all of life.

There is something powerful about this practice, which millions have used through Eastern Orthodoxy, through Hindu and Taoist meditation, and in the West through devotion to the Sacred Heart of Jesus. In our naked, silent intention, with our hearts open to God in Christ, we simply rest in God's presence, with the mind firmly established in the heart, standing before the Lord in awe, reverence, and devotion.

A technique that is used by those who practice the prayer of the heart is to intentionally bring to mind something that results in a softening of the heart towards God. As indicated in the first chapter, doing so can mean a remembrance of our sinfulness, gratitude for life's wonder and beauty, a current instance of suffering by or deep concern for ourselves or another, a sharp sense of desire and need for God, or anything else that awakens us to vulnerability.

One person may call to mind a recent instance of grief, loss, failure, or emotional perplexity. Another may remember a powerful sense of awe experienced at the beach or when looking at the night sky. Others might just call up into the present their genuine love for God and heart-felt desire to be more holy, more true. While this technique may seem artificial, if what is being recalled is actually part of one's real experience, it is real. The purpose here, however, is not to dwell on what is recalled. Instead, in a brief moment of vulnerability, we drop below our heads into our hearts.

Most of the time, we carry around a kind of emotional and spiritual shield, protecting ourselves from the world, in order that we not be too raw and sensitive. This is natural, and usually a good thing. But in prayer, we must let down these defenses, and stand before God vulnerably. In order for real contact, real loving intimacy to take place, we must become soft and real. Just as in any other intimate relationship, we cannot really make significant contact if we stay in our heads and remain well-defended. We must open our hearts. The brief calling to mind (and even naming before God) our humility, thankfulness, pain, desire, or dependence upon God is a way of warming the heart and melting the walls that stand before us. God wants us to be real, and warming the heart as we begin prayer is one way of doing so.

Having made vulnerable our hearts, we then do what we can to remain empty, open, expectant, doing nothing but loving God: no words, no intention, no thoughts or concerns other than being present in God's love. Remain in this place as long as you can. A familiar and oft-quoted Orthodox story tells of a parish priest who comes in and out of the church building each day and frequently notices an old man sitting there, just smiling. The priest, whose curiosity finally gets the better of him, asks the old man what he is doing. He replies "I look at God, God looks at me, and we are happy."

When you are praying with the heart and your mind tries to take control with a distraction, do not observe it, name it, or be otherwise concerned about it. This is not the time for *nepsis*. Just gently return to that place of open-hearted love for God. As you find yourself caught up in some concern or another, let go of it. This is the time for surrender, when we give up everything that is not God and our love for God. It is surrender because in this prayer, we give up everything that has to do with us and our busy, concerned lives. We surrender everything that we normally think defines us in life, and we do this in the moment of silent prayer by letting go of everything that attempts to get us engaged and take us away from simple presence.

This practice is a concrete way of experiencing what Jesus, St. Paul, and so many of the saints have described as "dying to self." We die to all our efforts and intentions and just sit before God with an open heart. We even die to our expectations of what this kind of prayer will feel like, or what it will result in for us. The prayer that prepares for the gift of contemplative union, rather than trying to maintain a feeling of peaceful, harmonic union with God, empties out all our expectations, distractions, and concerns, and just sits with an open heart before God, allowing God to use this time in whatever way is necessary. We die to self and allow God to live through us.

Perhaps you have had an experience of this kind of empty, open-hearted presence in your life. It seems to come as a gift, as a demonstration of God's life, when we get out of the way. In moments of extreme difficulty or sorrow, something just opens up and nothing else matters but being present. You are alive in God, and that is enough. At times when you are tired enough, stretched beyond what you think you can handle, your need to control the circumstances of your life just stops, and you let go into a wonderful place of peace. When your love for a wife, child, or other intimate rises up, all other concerns seem trivial by comparison, and you are able to be present to this one thing that you know is true.

Praying with the heart is like this. We surrender, and in surrendering we are opened to a greater reality. While we cannot create the dying to self and living to God that I describe here, we can clear the way for it, we can prepare the way for its coming. We can make the heart vulnerable and let go of everything that is not our love for God. We can practice a kind of dying to self and all that it wants, and just be before God.

This requires radical trust. Instead of trying to be peaceful, enlightened, or spiritually improved, we must die and be empty, waiting on God. Whatever life resurrects out of the ashes of the self is God's creation, not ours. To trust in the emptiness, rather than filling it with something we think is better, is truly radical faith. All we can do is be present with our hearts open wide, letting go of all that tries to close them, expectant and faithful, without any content to our expectations. We wait, hope, and have faith, but not for anything. We just wait, hope, and have faith.

This is the type of prayer that Thomas Keating and other proponents of centering prayer present. It is a wonderful practice, as long as we balance it by watching our minds and offering ourselves as we are to God. Heart-felt surrender, emptying, letting-go, and worship in union with God, as essential as this is, is not enough in itself. In contemplative prayer, we must also bring the purifying effort of repentance and will to bear, and we must come to self-awareness and the healing that results from illumination. And so to conclude, we bring together again the three strands of this chapter.

Will, Mind, and Heart together in Prayer

How do we know when we pray should by opening our hearts to God in loving worship, when we should focus our attention in a concentrated way, and when we should pray by watching and naming our thoughts through *nepsis*? There is no formulaic answer to these questions. It must be lived out in the years of a contemplative practice, hopefully with the companionship of a wise spiritual director and/or group of other seekers, since spiritual discernment of this sort requires great sensitivity.

At different times in our lives, one or the other approach to contemplative prayer may be more appropriate for us. A person who cannot just "open the heart" without feeling lost should learn first to focus more with a mantra or the breath. Someone who naturally feels God's loving presence in an empty, open way should probably just stay with that. Another who is assaulted by many thoughts and temptations in prayer should perhaps learn to step out of them mentally and name them, so to slow them down and take away some of their force. And once we have learned how to do each, it may be that on any given day, one way of praying may be more helpful than another. We can learn to shift from one to the other as needed.

But over time, we can also learn to flow gracefully from one to another in one period of prayer. We might begin with five minutes of concentrated attention to the body and breath, then spend five minutes watching what our mind is up to, and then spend the rest of our time letting go and opening to God in love.

In addition, it is possible to learn that these three ways of praying need not be done even at distinct and separate times, but can be held together as three strands of one prayerful experience. Just as purification, illumination, and union are three dimensions of our one life in God, they can also be three qualities of presence in one prayer.

Perhaps one day we notice in prayer that even though we are keenly aware of some personal drama of reactivity going on in the silence, we have not lost the sense of spaciousness in God. Both God and self remain present in one field of awareness. We learn to pray with a comprehensive awareness, with an open heart and a discerning mind, all the while remaining focused with all our effort. In a comprehensive way all at once, we love God with all our heart, all our mind, and all our strength.

One of the great delights of living in New Mexico is the Santa Fe Opera. Here, one sits in an open-air theater, watching the gripping, emotional operatic drama unfolding on stage. Men and women laugh, shout, fight, weep, murder and love. But at the same time, for the spectator there is always an awareness of the endless desert beyond, visibly stretching out for hundreds of miles. There is always the brilliant starry sky overhead.

Sitting in the vast, empty goodness of God's presence, we watch our small minds at work within a divine spaciousness. As if we are observing from a distance, the little operatic drama of our egocentric human lives is played out in the infinitely huge open air theater of love and peace, of breath and the liveliness of each instant. We will never be rid of this relatively little drama. As long as we are human, we will be affected by our early conditioning, and by the changes and chances of life.

But we can learn to experience it in the open air, so that even as we struggle in our humanity, we transcend ourselves in worship, knowing that all of it is contained within the sacred and infinite spaciousness of our Creator. Our contemplative prayer, then, can simultaneously include watching the mind and opening the heart to God. Prayer can be both awareness and surrender.

Above all, whether we are watching the reality of our small minds churning away or whether we are opening our hearts to God's mysterious presence, we must remember that all prayer is God's work far more than it is ours. The Spirit is actively at work in our depths, honoring our intentions to be available to God, working to transform us in ways of which we might not even be aware. Prayer is not a performance; it is not a technique that we can "master." Prayer is a relationship with the Holy One, who reaches out to us, and then responds to our responses. God makes possible in prayer what we cannot accomplish on our own efforts: union with the divine. Three of the masters in our contemplative tradition bear witness to this fact:

> The Spirit helps us in our weakness; for we do not know how to pray as we ought, but that very Spirit intercedes with sighs too deep for words.
> ~ St. Paul (Romans 8:26)

> If you want to pray, you need God, who gives prayer to one who prays.
> ~ Origen[13]

> Prayer has its own special teacher in God, who "teaches all the world knowledge" (Ps. 94:10). He grants the prayer of him who prays.
> ~ John Climacus[14]

---

13 Origen, An Exhortation to Martyrdom, Prayer and Selected Works, trans. Rowan A. Greer (New York: Paulist Press, 1979), 82.
14 John Climacus: The Ladder of Divine Ascent, trans. Colm Luibeheid and Norman Russell (New York: Paulist Press, 1982), 281.

Three

❧

Abiding in Christ

FOR CHRISTIANS, JESUS NORMALLY STANDS at the center of our faith lives. We are invited to be in relationship with him, and people approach this relationship in differing ways. Some see him as a wise and holy teacher, and do their best to follow him. Others relate to him simply as God, feeling that by his human form he is more accessible to them in prayer than the unseen Creator or Spirit. Many just accept what the church says about him, that he is the second person of the Trinity, the Son of God and Savior of the world, and leave it at that, without giving too much thought to what that means for them in their own faith experiences.

Christian contemplatives must also deal with Jesus at the center, as long as they practice their contemplation within the structure of the church, and their approaches to doing so are as varied as those of other Christians. Contemplatives, however, have a special opportunity to deepen their relationships with Jesus, by mining the rich treasures of the mystical perspective on Jesus. By mystical I do not mean some strange, visionary epiphany granted only to a few. I mean the wonderful, very real and yet completely inexplicable mystery of Christ's spiritual presence as resurrected spirit who dwells within us, guiding us and helping us mature into his likeness.

This mystical tradition extends back through our history as a church, into the scriptures themselves. Through this perspective, contemplatives can develop a relationship with Christ that is based not primarily upon doctrine or imitative behavior, but upon a direct experience of his indwelling spirit. In this chapter I will begin with a brief introduction to one of the New Testament themes that serves as a foundation for this experiential relationship, and then outline several traditional practices of Jesus-centered prayer that build upon this foundation.

The mystical perspective on Christ begins with the belief that Jesus fully experienced union with God ("I and the Father are one." John 10:30). Jesus also claimed that through an intimate relationship with him, his followers would know the same unity ("The glory that you have given me I have given them, so that they may be one, as we are one, I in them and you in me." John 17:22-23). The way in which the contemplative Christian comes to experience this divine unity and this glory is by abiding *in Christ*. Through the intimacy of his indwelling, Jesus takes us with him into the presence of God.

Jesus will forever seem remote and vague until we develop some sort of immediate relationship with him. We can believe certain theological doctrines about him, we can admire and follow his teachings, but until we know him, until we live in him and he lives in us, we will remain relatively unaffected by him. When we abide with him, we know him, and when we know him, he takes us into the fulness of God's life, which he promised.

Throughout the Gospels, but especially in John, we can see the early church inviting us into this kind of intimate relationship with Jesus, using a wide variety of images. His birth is heralded as God with us. He claims that he will be with us always, to the end of the age. He said when we eat his eucharistic flesh and drink his blood, we abide in him, and that by abiding in him we abide in God. He said that we share in his and in God's life by entering into him as the gate, the light, the bread of heaven, living water, and the true vine. He prayed that we would be one with him and with God as he was one with God, sharing in the same glory.

Paul speaks of being baptized into Christ's death and resurrection, of dying and being reborn in him. He says that it is no longer Paul who lives, but Christ in him. He calls us joint heirs with Christ in adoption as children of God. He claims that nothing in this world can separate us from the love of God in Christ Jesus. He says that we are living members of Christ's body. He says that we have the mind of Christ.

Further, the author of Colossians says that as in Christ the fullness of divinity dwells, so we have come to fullness in him, and are to be revealed with him in his glory. In the second letter of Peter, the author even says that in Christ we become participants in the divine nature.

This is, I believe, what these early Christians meant by having faith in Jesus, believing in him: not belief in the sense of agreeing to certain exclusive theological assertions about him, but placing our trust in him. We place our trust in him by calling upon him, inviting him to live within, believing that his way will lead us to life, allowing him to gradually become more and more of a presence to the point where he becomes us, that is, he lives his life through us, and he takes us into the fullness of God.

Pseudo-Macarius wrote about this mystical process of faith as mutual indwelling in a homily on the story of Martha and Mary.[1] He says that Jesus spoke words that endowed Mary with a hidden, "in-breathing" power from his very being to hers:

---

1 Martha, who was busy playing host to the disciples, complained about how Mary would not help her, but sat instead at the feet of Jesus, listening to him. While women in particular might have real sympathy with Martha's point of view, Jesus commends Mary for her prayerful attentiveness, and the story has been used ever since as a paradigm of the contemplative call (Luke 10:38-42.).

These words penetrated her heart and brought his soul to her soul, his Spirit to her spirit, and a divine power filled her heart. That power, necessarily, wherever it is released, remains there as a possession which cannot be taken away.[2]

Contemplative prayer is one way that we can learn to "abide with Christ," as the New Testament calls it, becoming filled with the divine power of his soul. Contemplation is a way of placing our faith in Jesus, inviting his mystical presence and relying on him to live his life through us. And it is a way in which we can come to know, through the power of his presence, something of the same union with God that he knows. We continue, then, with some specific ways in which we can learn to abide with him contemplatively, and be transformed by his presence.

The Jesus Prayer

One ancient Christian discipline of contemplation that offers a concrete way of abiding in Christ is the Eastern Orthodox practice of the Jesus Prayer. This is the repetition of the phrase, "Lord Jesus Christ, Son of God, have mercy on me, a sinner." It is often reduced to "Lord Jesus, have mercy" or some other variation. At the very least, just the name "Jesus" is invoked.

The repetition of this phrase is used in various ways. It can be invoked from time to time in prayer, as a kind of spiritual re-start button, bringing us back to focus. One can use it repetitively as a mantra throughout a period of contemplative prayer. It can be utilized for brief periods during the day in order to enter into prayer as one drives a car, waits in line, or sits in a meeting. Or it can become a constant voice in the heart, gradually increasing in

---

2 *Pseudo-Macarius*, Maloney, 103.

usage until it is always there in the background all long. One of its advantages is that as we build an association with its use in deep prayer, we can use it as a quick and familiar trigger to help us drop deeply into prayer, at any time, at any place.

The tradition teaches, first of all, that we begin a period of contemplation using the Jesus Prayer with a request for God to assist we in even being able to pray. Recognizing the presence of the Spirit, we remember that God wants us to pray well, and stands ready to help us in doing so. And so we begin by asking for God's grace to lead us into true prayer, to help us be awake and devoted with all our heart.

As outlined in the previous chapter, the fathers of this tradition then ask us to soften our hearts, to become vulnerable to God. We do this by recalling before God something that we feel deeply about: a beautiful and moving moment, something about which we feel badly, a special need of our own or another, or our gratitude for God's love and goodness. Tears may come; in fact, the Eastern fathers recommend it! They also recommend a "warming" of the heart, which may have something to do with the increased amount of conscious energy we focus in this region of our bodies. With the heart less defended and made softer, warmer, and humbler, we are more prepared to be real with God.

Then it is customary to spend a few moments in intercession or petition: praying for others or for ourselves. This is a way of holding before God the particular needs we and others have in life, so that as contemplatives, our prayer does not become overly spiritualized and removed from the realities of everyday life. When we begin our prayer this way it also has the effect of clearing our mind a bit, so that we might be less apt to spend our time in contemplation by mulling over things we are concerned about.

The Jesus Prayer is then repeated silently, in synch with the breath. On the inhale, say "Lord Jesus Christ" and on the exhale, say "have mercy on me." A shorter version might be "Lord Jesus…have mercy." Pause at the end of the exhale before inhaling and repeating the phrase again, in order to rest in a little silent, still space.

Some people are put off by the seemingly penitential nature of the words "have mercy" and, in the longer form of the prayer, "upon me, a sinner." While these phrases certainly can be understood penitentially, and there are times for that in our lives, they need not be. To ask for mercy doesn't necessarily mean "please don't strike me dead even though I deserve it!" Mercy is simply the attention and the goodness of God. When we ask for it, we ask that God turn towards us and be gracious. When we call ourselves a sinner, it does not necessarily mean that we are a terrible failure of a human being. Saying that we are a sinner is another way of saying that we are imperfect and human, and that we know that we cannot ascend on our own into union with God. We are imperfect and lowly, in comparison with the Holy One whom we humbly seek. And so to say "have mercy on me a sinner" can mean "I need your goodness, because I am merely human."

As you repeat the phrase, develop a sense that you are entering into the intention of the words: to call upon the presence of Jesus, to be present to one another. Feel this desire, simply to be lovingly attentive to Christ. Let this desire be the one thing you intend in this prayer. Let this intention sink down out of your head into your softened heart. As your chest moves up and down with the breath, sense your heart beating. The breath, the beating of the heart, and your desire to be lovingly attentive to Jesus: all of this is one simple experience in the silence of the moment.

Linking the phrase with the breath and the warmth of the heart is a way of making our prayer not just mental but also physical. Another way of making this link is through the use of a prayer rope (called a *komboschoinion* in Greek, a *tchotki* in Russian), consisting of a knotted black wool rope with fifty or one hundred knots and a cross.

You hold a knot of the prayer rope between thumb and index finger as you say the Jesus Prayer phrase with the breath, then move the rope so that you hold the next knot for the next repetition of the phrase. A string of beads, even a rosary, can work just as well. Sometimes I find that the use of the rope helps integrate body and mind in a more focused way. Other times it becomes a distraction, too much movement, and I prefer to be physically still.

In this tradition there is also the physical practice of *metanoias* ("turning," or "repenting"), a bowing practice. The greater *metanoia* is made by bowing at the waist and then and lowering yourself to the floor on your knees and touching your head to the floor. The lesser one is made by simply bowing from the waist.

Metanoias are done as ways of integrating the body into prayer, and expressing our humility, devotion, and surrender to God. It is quite possible that this practice of greater *metanoias* in the Eastern early church was something that predated and influenced its use in Islamic prayer. Both religious traditions practice it to this day in the Middle East. Done occasionally, at the beginning and/or the end of our prayer time, bowing can be a powerful way of expressing humble, devotional prayer with the whole being.

The tradition then teaches us that as ordinary, passing thoughts come and go, temporarily taking our attention with them, we should let them go. See if thoughts can become more transparent, less gripping. Treat them almost like clouds floating past you in a vast blue sky. Your life in Christ is like the sky, and all the concerns of the self are like the clouds, drifting by. Let them drift.

The patristic and Eastern fathers teach us also to practice *nepsis,* watching the mind, as more gripping thoughts and emotional reactions take hold of you. In this case, stop and recognize what your mind is doing. Name the thought before Christ. Let him in on what you are up to. Hold your attachment or your fear or whatever it is as a sacred offering to Christ, an offering of who you are in this moment. There is no shame, no judgment, only the humility of an honest offering of self-awareness. Guard your softened heart by watching the mind. Inquire of the thought its business there, name it and momentarily feel its energy, then return to worship, using the name of Jesus again (a fuller treatment of *nepsis* is found in the previous chapter).

If real stillness (*hesychia*) comes, just drop the words and be still in God's presence. This is the gift of contemplation, and it is given by God from time to time. The Eastern fathers teach us that at this point, the words of the Jesus Prayer have done their work, and it is no longer necessary to repeat them. Just be still and know that God is. Remain in this place of union for as long as it lasts. As the stillness disperses again, like ripples in a smooth pond when a stone is dropped in it, return to the use of the Jesus Prayer.

At the end of the time of prayer, offer some prayers of thanksgiving, gratitude, and self-dedication, either in memorized or spontaneous form.

Here, then, is a summary of this practice for your reference:

- Begin with full or partial bows, if this is helpful to you
- Ask for God's help in being able to pray well
- Soften and warm your heart;
- Pray for specific needs;
- Use the Jesus Prayer, opening your heart in love to God;

- Use a prayer rope or beads in the recitation of the prayer, if this is helpful;
- As strong thoughts capture your attention, watch, name, feel, and offer them to God;
- If stillness comes, stop using words and just be present to God;
- As stillness disperses, return to the Jesus Prayer;
- Conclude your time of prayer with thanksgiving, gratitude and self-dedication;
- End with full or partial bows, if it seems right;

As you learn to practice this form of prayer, one of the things that happens is that everything you associate with Jesus will gradually saturate the prayer and your intention in using it. His teachings about the blessedness of peacemakers, his love for the poor, his healing presence, his ability to name injustice and evil without slipping into hatred, his utter trust in the immediacy and goodness of God, his unconditional love for everyone...all this and everything else you associate with Jesus will be contained in the invocation of his name.

In this sense the Jesus Prayer becomes a way in which we become Christ, or he becomes us. For Jesus' name itself has an energy, a force to it that invokes all that Jesus is. Through the use of Jesus' name, his being soaks into our being; we become more like him. In this regard the ninth century monk Hesychius of Sinai wrote:

> The more the rain falls on the earth, the softer it makes it; similarly, the more we call upon Christ's holy Name, the greater the rejoicing and exultation it brings to the earth of our heart.[3]

But this is not all. Just as Jesus was attuned to all God's children and to all of life, the repeated invocation of his holy name moves us into a similar harmony with other

---

3 Quoted by Clement, *The Roots of Christian Mysticism*, 241.

people, with all creation. The author of *The Way of A Pilgrim* described how he was affected by this saturation in the name of Jesus, how he began to take on Jesus' own perspective, Jesus' own life:

> Everybody was kind to me, it was as though everyone loved me...The trees, the grass, the birds, the earth, the air, the light seemed to be telling me that they existed for man's sake, that they witnessed to the love of God for man, that everything proved the love of God for man, that all things prayed to God and sang his praise...
> I felt a burning love for Jesus and for all God's creatures.[4]

At this point, it may be useful to know how this simple yet powerful, ancient form of Christian contemplative prayer came into being, in order to foster some appreciation and respect for its depth and breadth. For we Western Christians tend to be tragically isolated from and ignorant of the riches of our Eastern brothers and sisters, just as they are from us.

In the West, we have emphasized individual freedom of expression when it comes to prayer, and as a result, we have no long-term experience with or body of writings about any particular contemplative discipline. In the East, by contrast, a precious heritage consisting of a specific approach to contemplation, based upon the Jesus Prayer, has been handed down faithfully from master to disciple, and is carefully preserved in a much-venerated body of writings, *The Philokalia* (in the East, this collection is considered second only to the Bible).

It is not known when the use of this ancient prayer became firmly established, but it is clear that the roots of its development go back to the first centuries of Eastern

---

4 *The Way of a Pilgrim*, trans. R.M. French (New York: Seabury, 1965), 85.

monasticism. Early on, a phrase from the psalms, such as "O God, make haste to save me," was used as a short invocation to God, repeated from time to time in order to focus the mind in contemplative prayer. This phrase is still preferred to the name of Jesus in some places of the East, out of a sense of humility. However, at some point these desert contemplatives began to use the name of Jesus as their invocation. In the fourth century text *The Life of Anthony*, by Athanasius of Alexandria, there was already a practice of invoking Christ in repetitive prayer, even linking the breath to its repetition, as if the one who prayed was actually breathing Jesus:

> Anthony called his two companions…and said to them, "Always breathe Christ."[5]

In the fifth century *Coptic Cycle of Sayings*, Pseudo-Macarius says, in a passage utilizing the image of a ship anchored to a rock:

> The ship is your heart; keep guard over it. The rope is your mind; secure it to our Lord Jesus Christ, who is the rock who has power over all the waves…because it is not difficult, is it, to say with each breath, "Our Lord Jesus, have mercy on me: I bless you, my Lord Jesus, help me."[6]

In the seventh century, John Climacus advised:

> Let your calling to mind of Jesus be continually combined with your breathing and you will know the meaning of silence.
> ~ *The Ladder of Divine Ascent*, 27th Step[7]

Eventually the phrase we now know as the Jesus Prayer became normative. The practice of its repetition was seen as a way of continually calling on Christ's presence,

---

5 Clement, *The Roots of Christian Mysticism*, 204.
6 Ibid., 205.
7 Ibid., 204.

in order to better abide in him. Over time, a whole tradition of very specific teachings about contemplative prayer developed, with the Jesus Prayer at its center. I outlined some of the broader themes of this practice of this tradition in the previous chapter, with its emphases of concentration, *nepsis* (watching the mind), and the prayer of the heart.

This rich and focused tradition is perhaps the only specific, practical teaching about contemplative prayer in all of Christendom that has been handed down faithfully and precisely from master to disciple, remaining intact over sixteen hundred years. In this sense, the Jesus Prayer/Prayer of the Heart tradition is more akin to the way in which Buddhist or Hindu meditation is handed down from generation to generation than it is to anything comparable in the West.

The use of the Jesus Prayer and the teachings about contemplation that surrounded it spread from master to disciple through the deserts of Egypt, and then came into prominence in the sixth century at the well-known and ancient monastery of St. Catherine on Mt. Sinai, established by Emperor Justinian I in 527. In the fourteenth century the center of the Jesus Prayer movement moved to Mt. Athos, Greece. Mt. Athos is actually a narrow peninsula, upon which the only buildings and activities are those of numerous monasteries and hermitages, and it is a self-governing state of Greece. In our day, Mt. Athos and to a lesser degree, St. Catherine's of Sinai, continue as centers of practice of the Jesus Prayer.

---

8 *The Philokalia* has been translated into English, so far, in five volumes. The first of these is a selection of writings taken from Bishop Theophan's Russian version, containing passages from *The Philokalia* specific to the Jesus Prayer/Prayer of the Heart, and is perhaps the most approachable: *Writings from the Philokalia on Prayer of the Heart*, trans. E. Kadloubovsky and G.E.H. Palmer (London: Faber and Faber, 1951). The full Philokalia is still in the process of

In the eighteenth century, a monk from Mt. Athos (St. Nikodimos, together with St. Makarios of Corinth) compiled writings from the fourth to the fifteenth centuries on this contemplative tradition, which resided in the libraries of the various Athonite monasteries. This invaluable collection was published in Greek in 1782 as *The Philokalia* ("the love of spiritual beauty"). Shortly afterwards, *The Philokalia* came to the attention of a Russian monk, Paisii Velichkovskii, who translated it into Slavonic. In the mid-nineteenth it was translated into Russian in two different versions by the Bishops Ignatius Brianchaninov and Theophan the Recluse.[8]

By this point, the fame of *The Philokalia* had spread, which inspired the writing and publication in 1884 of *The Way of the Pilgrim*. This book chronicled the journey through Russia of a seeker who devoted himself to the practice of the Jesus Prayer and the reading of *The Philokalia*, and it rapidly found enormous popular success. Here was a simple and inspirational description of the contemplative life from the perspective of the average uneducated lay person. Since the time of the publication of *The Way of The Pilgrim*, the Jesus Prayer has been well-known among all Eastern Orthodox, and more recently, in the West as well.

For contemplatives, the use of the Jesus Prayer may be one of the most ancient, consistently taught, simplest, most direct, and powerful ways of accessing Christ's transformative presence in prayer. It calls upon us only to be present, to open our hearts to God, and to observe those personal obstacles that arise to stand in the way of that openness. By using the name of Jesus, it encap-

---

being translated into English from the original Greek version by Ss. Nikodimos and Makarios (four volumes of this series have been published, and a final fifth is in preparation): *The Philokalia, the Complete Text Volumes I-IV*, trans. eds. G.E.H. Palmer, Philip Sherrard, Kallistos Ware (London: Faber and Faber, 1979, 1981, 1984, 1995).

sulates everything we know, believe, love, and hope about him, who is both the human face of God as well as our human potential. But rather than thinking about Jesus or our relationship to him, the Jesus Prayer brings us into his very presence. We call upon him, and he draws near. And in this nearness, he lives his life through us and takes us into the glory of God.

Lectio Divina

Christians, and Jews before them, have always had a reverence for the effect of reading scripture. It has always been recognized that the Word of God is a living Word. It transforms the hearers, if they are listening prayerfully. Monks, from the earliest desert origins, learned to meditate, to chew on scripture throughout the day. They memorized psalms and other passages, letting the living force of the Spirit work through the words into their souls, where they would be converted by the Word. The desert father Abba Poemen is said to have commented (keep in mind here that fear of God has more to do with awe than being scared):

> The nature of water is soft, that of stone is hard; but if a bottle is hung above the stone, allowing the water to fall drop by drop, it wears away the stone. So it is with the Word of God; it is soft and our heart is hard, but the one who hears the Word of God often, opens his heart to the fear of God.[9]

Lectio divina, or divine reading, comes from this monastic practice of pondering and living prayerfully with a passage of scripture. In this method of prayer, one moves naturally from hearing to responding, and then to an empty, open contemplating.

---

9 The Sayings of the Desert Fathers, Ward, 192.

It may not seem as if *lectio* has much to do with contemplation, if we think of silent prayer standing alone by itself, without any intellectual reflection or devotional prayers. But Christian contemplation is always practiced in the context of traditional resources that balance, challenge, and support us. These resources include Holy Scripture, the sacraments, the community of faith, theology, service to those in need, and various spiritual disciplines. Without this context, we are always in the danger of an overly privatized approach to prayer that inevitably leads us out on a long, narrow, strange limb.

With these traditional resources, our spiritual life, even our silent contemplative practice, is grounded in something substantial, true, and tested by time. *Lectio* with scripture helps us pray well contemplatively, because it provides a broad, wise, dependable foundation upon which our contemplation can be grounded, and from which we can enter safely into the mystery of God. For beginning contemplatives especially, the practice of *lectio* provides a much-needed structure that helps one move into contemplative silence. Without this kind of structure, sometimes beginners feel a bit at a loss as to how to jump into the silent, divine emptiness!

For our purposes of learning to abide in Christ, it is best in our *lectio* to select a passage from one of the Gospels. A *pericope*, that is, a passage that can stand alone as a story or saying, will do, as will a shorter passage, even one sentence.[10] Begin by reading it slowly, carefully. The first phase of *lectio* is the use of the mind:

---

10 In the Episcopal Church's *Book of Common Prayer*, there is a Daily Office Lectionary in the back (beginning on p. 934 with instructions about how to use it) which assigns three readings and several psalms to each day. The advantages of using this or a similar lectionary is that you will be following the liturgical cycles of the church year, you will be less likely to limit your *lectio* only to pre-ferred and comfortable passages, and you will be joining with thousands of others who are reading the same readings on the same days.

listen carefully to the passage. Before jumping into what the text might be saying *to you,* consider first what the text is actually *saying.* What is the author's point? What is the audience, the message, the tenor of the passage? How does it fit in the context of what is around it? Then especially, in a Jesus-centered form of lectio, who is Jesus? What is he like? What kind of figure is the author of this particular gospel presenting Jesus to be? How does he speak to those around him in this passage? How do others respond to him?

After looking objectively at the text, then look at it subjectively: how does it speak to you now? Remember that the Bible is the living Word, that it has an active spiritual power to engage us, speak to us, and guide us. Through the meditation of your mind on the Gospel passage, let Jesus say something to you that might reflect on your own current life situation. How does Jesus challenge, comfort, or puzzle you? How might he be asking you to see differently your life circumstances right now?

This gives way, naturally, to the next phase of *lectio:* our prayerful response to what may have come up for us in our meditation on the passage. Let this form itself into a verbal prayer to Christ. While our meditation involves the use of the mind, verbal prayer may move more into our emotions. Here we allow Jesus into our longing, our guilt, our passion, our need for guidance, our confusion, despair, or desire. We may pray for clarity, or for forgiveness. We may pray that Jesus, through his indwelling presence, gives us the strength to move forward in faith. We may just offer thanksgiving.

After forming the prayer that is a response to meditation, *lectio* flows naturally into the final phase, contemplation. Here we sit with Christ in an empty, open availablity. Whatever insights we have had in meditating on the passage, whatever prayer has then emerged, now we sit in silence with Jesus, inviting his transformative life to do its work in us. This is the movement into faith, where we are not in control. As helpful as intellectual insight and emotional expression can be in prayer, it is silent contemplation that is really the work of faith. For in contemplation, as we rest in Christ, we simply trust his hidden presence to be at work in ways that we cannot and do not have to see. This might be a good time to use the Jesus Prayer in our contemplation.

An example of how this might look using a specific passage from the Gospels would be the following. Let us say that the assigned reading for the day is the passage in Mark, chapter 11, where Jesus enters the temple in Jerusalem, driving out the money-changers. First, we read the passage carefully and slowly. Then, we begin to look at its content objectively. We ask ourselves what could have made Jesus as angry as he was. We try to see things from the perspectives of the disciples, who might have been astonished at Jesus; or the money-changers, who may have thought they were only providing a useful religious purpose for pilgrims coming to worship; or the authorities, who saw in Jesus a very real threat to civil order. We remember that prior to this passage, Jesus was hailed as the Son of David in his triumphant Palm Sunday entrance into the city, and we think ahead to the betrayal, arrest, and crucifixion. Perhaps we wonder about the connection between these two events and his angry cleansing of the temple.

Then we shift to the ways in which this passage might be speaking personally to us. How might Jesus express divine rage about injustice in our lives or in the world around us? How does Jesus call us to join him in reacting to injustice in our lives? How are we like the authorities, trying to clamp a lid on anything that threatens comfort and order in our lives or our workplace?

We then let something arise that speaks to us more emphatically than anything else, and turn it into a prayer. We might say something like one of the following: "Lord Jesus, give me courage to speak out against the unfairness in my office, to do something about it...help me to receive your judgment of my life without shame or fear...give me clearer discernment about this situation that troubles me, that doesn't seem right, so that I might act faithfully."

After offering our prayer that arises out of meditation, we then begin a time of contemplation, not holding on to what we have reflected upon, but letting go of it, knowing that if there needs to be some connection with our meditation and our contemplation, God will accomplish it for us. A simple recitation of the Jesus Prayer can be one way of resting in Christ during this time of contemplation.

Praying with *lectio divina,* using a pericope from the Gospels as our text, is a powerful way of being in a dynamic relationship with Jesus. We can hear his words in church or skim over them in a cursory reading of the Bible without ever being touched by them. But to really take the time to listen to Jesus is another matter altogether. At a difficult time in our lives we hear him say to us, "Come to me, all who labor and are heavy laden, and I will give you rest." And so we come and rest. When we think we're pretty successful and we've got life pretty much under control, he tells us that we can gain the whole world and lose our souls, and we are cut to the quick. When we are self-righteously angry and feeling retributive about some perceived injustice against us, he says, "Pray for those who persecute you." When we feel ashamed of ourselves, we read the story of the father's unconditional forgiveness of the prodigal son.

Christ is present to us today in our prayerful absorption in the Gospels. He reaches out to us through his living Word, touches, challenges, and changes us. *Lectio* can bring us some objective content, beyond our own subjectivity, to our relationship with Jesus. *Lectio* thus helps us move out of an overly personal, limited way of praying, and into a more balanced view. In doing *lectio* with various passages of the Gospels over time, it gives us the broader perspective of things we would not normally think about on our own. It widens the base of our foundation for prayer. When we prayerfully listen to what he has to say to us, we relate to him on his terms, not ours. Jesus is the way, the truth, and the life, expressed to us today in complete love. Opening to his objective truth, we are led by him on the way, into his life.

Then in our silent, empty, and open contemplation, we invite him, after having had an encounter with him on his own terms, to quietly transform us by his presence. It is as if we have just had an intense conversation with our very wise beloved, where we are exposed, delighted, or forgiven. We then we lie quietly in one another's arms. There is healing in this wordless, contemplative presence with one another.

A summary of the practice of a Jesus-based *lectio divina* would then look like this:

- Begin with a prayerful, slow reading of the Gospel passage;
- Reflect on its objective content, context, and message;
- Meditate subjectively about what it says to you and your life circumstances;
- Let a prayer emerge out of this meditation;
- Move into contemplative, silent prayer, perhaps using the Jesus Prayer.

Lectio can be an excellent way of beginning or ending our time of contemplative prayer. As a beginning, it sets our orientation God-ward, and moves us naturally from reflection and verbal prayer into contemplation. As an ending, we find our minds and hearts newly, differently open to scripture after having first slowed down and spent some time in contemplative silence.

The practice of *lectio divina* can also be combined with the use of the Daily Office.[11] One can choose to pray one or more of these daily as a broader context for lectio, expanding the office to include some time for reading, meditating, and praying with the appointed lessons for the day, and then moving into a time of contemplation. After doing this lectio and contemplation, then return to the completion of the office.

Praying with Icons

Another Jesus-centered contemplative practice is prayer with an icon, a traditionally painted represen-tation of Jesus. While a real icon is best, even a printed reproduction of one will do. Remember that an icon is meant to function as a window, through which the one who prays before it may be taken into Jesus' real presence. The spiritual gaze of faith is not meant to stop with the icon, but to penetrate the icon's depth and then open into the subject it represents.

Set the icon up in front of where you meditate, perhaps with a candle near it. Its location should be where your eyes will fall at a forty-five degree angle down in front of you. During contemplation, gaze into Jesus' eyes and hold your attention there throughout the duration of your time of prayer.[12]

Use the time of meditation as a time to simply sit in Jesus' presence, to soak up his being. Do not think about

---

11 In the Episcopal *Book of Common Prayer* there are four daily offices, or short services of prayer, taken originally from the monastic tradition, meant to be said on a daily basis (see pp. 35–146).

12 I am aware that for most Orthodox Christians, icons are usually used as a background presence. They are kissed, bowed to, and felt as a presence in the room during worship or private prayer. The Orthodox tend not to gaze contemplatively at them for periods of time as I suggest here.

his life, his teachings, or what you might say to him. Just sit with him. Open your heart to Jesus and let him be present to you. As always, your mind will wander during this kind of open-ended contemplation. That is fine. Whenever you discover that it has, just bring it back to the gaze that you share with Christ. Bring it back to the moment at hand, where you sit with him. Use his eyes as a way of knowing the experience that God is always present to us, always seeing all, always wanting us.

Over a period of time as we gaze into the eyes of a Jesus icon, as our minds wander in and out of attentiveness to him, we may discover that his unwavering presence becomes a gripping motivation for us to stay in the present moment with him. There is, after all, a kind of accountability to staying present when someone is looking, unwaveringly, at you. When someone is looking deeply into your eyes, it is hard to go to sleep, or to look out the window and start whistling a distracting tune. In the gaze of prayer with Jesus, he may even start to become startlingly present to us, pulling us more deeply into the moment. Our hearts open to God, we sit in the electricity of the now. Not knowing how long it will last, or where this electrified moment with God will take us, we remain committed to it, for whatever purposes God might use it.

On the other hand, to sit gazing into Jesus' eyes may be quite restful. His presence may be calming, like a loving mother who simply gazes into the eyes of her infant. In fact, there are other parallels between iconic prayer and mother-infant bonding. Both are wordless communications of being. Both are ways in which the less mature becomes shaped by the other. Both are exchanges of being, where the essence of one slowly becomes a part of the other. Both are ways in which an enormous amount of subconscious material moves back and forth.

Gazing into the eyes of a Jesus icon can also be disturbing. For one who has been the victim of sexual abuse, it may be too much of a recreation of someone who intruded, who crossed intimate boundaries through a stare. Prayer with an icon is not helpful or safe for everyone.

This wide variety of responses to eye-gazing with an icon of Jesus is possible, in part, because in classic iconography, the figures are neutral in their expressions. They have a serious look, but it does not communicate anything too specific. While some prefer a drawing of Jesus laughing, expressing joy, the icon is more like the Mona Lisa, so neutral as to be capable of taking on whatever the viewer needs it to be. If what we need is joy, then we see a quiet, serious joy. If we need the truth of God's judgment, then we may see sternness. If what we need is Christ to share in our suffering, then we see that, too, in the eyes. If we need love, then we are able to receive love in Jesus' gaze.

The icon also has the appearance of looking at us. This is because in traditional iconography, the perspective is reversed. In representational paintings, the viewer is the subject who looks at the object of the painting, which recedes away from the viewer as it diminishes. In a traditional icon, the painting's perspective seems to gain in width as it goes back, so that the viewer is the object, being viewed by the painting itself. We are being seen by Christ.

This offers us a profound lesson about prayer: that Christ sees us, knows us, and prays through us. Prayer is not just up to us. When we pray in faith before an icon, our spiritual gaze penetrates through the icon to Jesus' actual presence. But Christ's gaze also penetrates us. His life enters into ours.

Even though in the following passage he was not speaking of icons, Pseudo-Macarius nevertheless addresses what happens when we fix our gaze on Jesus, and he fixes his gaze on us. He uses the metaphor of a painter and his model who keep their attention focused on one another, in order that the painter might create an image:

> In a similar way the good portrait painter, Christ, for those who believe in him and gaze continually toward him, at once paints according to his own image a heavenly man. It is necessary that we gaze on [Jesus], believing and loving him, casting aside all else and attending to him so that he may paint his own heavenly image and send it into our souls.
> ~ *Homily* 30.4[13]

Eating His Body, Drinking His Blood

In the eucharist, or the mass, the church has developed a public, liturgical way of expressing and embracing our mystical union with Christ. Through a contemplative approach to this sacrament, we find another powerful way of abiding in Christ.

The eucharist is not merely a remembrance of what happened at the Last Supper two thousand years ago. It is a re-enactment, a making present of that encounter with Jesus. In this encounter, Jesus said to his disciples, as he says to us today in the eucharist, that he is really with us in our sharing of bread and wine in his name. As if to underscore the reality of this mystical presence, he uses the most graphic terms imaginable. He does not say that when we eat bread and drink wine we will remember him. He says, "Take, eat, this is my body," and "Drink this, all of you, this is my blood." He says, "Those who eat my flesh and drink my blood abide in me and I in them."

These sayings, expressed so bluntly in the most shocking forms imaginable, were intended to wake us up to an inconceivable reality. The sharing of eucharistic

---

13 *Pseudo-Macarius*, Maloney, 191.

bread and wine is an actual physical, spiritual, emotional, and intellectual encounter with Jesus in the here and now. This thought is still shocking. When we examine how blithely we usually saunter up to receive communion, as if we are being handed some innocuous spiritual vitamin, we can see we seldom take seriously this very real encounter with Jesus of Nazareth.

To say that we are eating his flesh and drinking his blood is to say that his being is being poured out into us, that we mingle his being with ours. As we invite his heart, mind, and body into our hearts, minds, and bodies, he mixes his life with ours. He becomes us, and we become him. *Abide in me, and I in you*, he said. Our bodies, our beings, become a temple of his presence.

This is why St. Paul spoke to Christians so vehemently against sexual immorality. "Do you not know that your bodies are members of Christ? Should I therefore take the members of Christ and make them members of a prostitute? Never!" (1 Cor. 6:15). The same thing could be said about any other form of abuse toward ourselves or others, be it physical, mental, or emotional. Disrespect for self and others is disrespect for Christ, if we are one with him.

In the eucharist, we celebrate and enter into the mystical union that Jesus promised to us. To receive communion with awareness is a profoundly contemplative act. For in this act, we are simply saying yes to Jesus' living in us, whatever that may mean. We invite him again into our lives, asking him to be in the depths of our hearts, and to do whatever he needs to do to transform us. As such it is an act of incredible trust. Because it is an open, completely intimate invitation to union, it is a contemplative action. Because we cannot exert any control whatsoever on the effect of Jesus' presence within us, it is the ultimate in contemplative faith.

What comes of this encounter? Of course Jesus will give us comfort and healing when it is needed. But he will also lead us into transformation of life, which can include pain, paradox, struggle, and unknowing mystery. This is also the same Jesus who exposed hypocrisy, silenced all self-justification, died on the cross, and rose triumphant over death itself. When we willingly, knowingly invite this presence to live more fully in us, we are saying yes to a process that leads us into complete transformation, via the way of the cross.

For contemplatives, it is one thing to learn to open to God in silent, trusting prayer. For the Christian contemplative, it is another thing to learn to open to Jesus. For Jesus not only takes us on the challenging and life-changing way of the cross and resurrection that he trod, he leads us into the same union with God that he knew. He takes our daily prayerful invitation to live in us seriously. We ask him to abide in us, and he does. Through contemplative practices such as the Jesus Prayer, *lectio* with the Gospels, prayer with an icon, and eucharistic devotion, he not only comes to us; he abides in us continually, transforming us into his likeness. This means that over time, he becomes us. We become Christ.

The tenth century abbot of a monastery in Constantinople, Symeon the New Theologian, expressed this in one of his remarkable hymns:

> We awaken in Christ's body as Christ awakens
> our bodies,
> and my poor hand is Christ's.
> He enters my foot, and is infinitely me.
>
> I move my hand and wonderfully my hand
> becomes Christ,
> becomes all of him
> (for God is indivisibly whole, seamless in
> his Godhead).

I move my foot, and at once
he appears like a flash of lightning.
Do my words seem blasphemous?
Then open your heart to him.

And let yourself receive the one
who is opening to you so deeply.
For if we genuinely love him,
we wake up inside Christ's body.

Where all our body, all our every most
hidden part of it,
is realized in joy as him,
and he makes us utterly real.

And everything that is hurt,
everything that seemed to us dark, harsh,
shameful,
maimed, ugly, irreparably damaged,
is in him transformed.

And recognized as whole, as lovely
and radiant in his light,
we awaken as the Beloved,
in every last part of our body.

❀

Part Two: Context

A REGULAR PRACTICE OF CONTEMPLATIVE prayer is challenging for anyone who undertakes it. We sometimes get bored, find ourselves lacking stimulation and direction, and at times we lose our way. To move as pilgrims towards an agenda-free, open-hearted encounter with the living God is a potentially overwhelming thing. It is a journey into a sacred mystery, beyond the limitations of our small world-views, beyond our limited capacities to comprehend.

This is why we must set our private practice of contemplative prayer within the larger context of the church's life. The contemplative needs the church's saints, sacraments, community, spiritual directors, traditional disciplines, scripture, theology, and other seekers. We need experienced guides, companions, maps, and signposts. We need food for the journey.

The chapters that follow explore many ways in which the rich tradition and resources of the church can support a private practice of contemplative prayer. For me, this support has been critical for the long haul and has removed from my shoulders the burden of continually renewing and maintaining something I cannot do on my own. This context has also proved to be a source of great joy and discovery, the end of which I will never reach in this lifetime.

Four

❈

The Contemplative in the Church

THE FIRST SECTION OF THIS BOOK is concerned with the development of a practice of contemplative prayer. This is primary, for we can only look at contemplation from the inside out, by becoming people of prayer. And as Thomas Merton said, "If you want a life of prayer, the way to get to it is by praying."[1]

Now it is time to consider the essential context for that life of prayer, which is, for the Christian, in one form or another, the church and her tradition that is embodied in worship, teaching, community, and service. I believe this context is essential for all Christians who seek spiritual growth and maturity, for several reasons. The first is that community is something basic to the very nature of Christianity. Secondly, left on our own, it is all too possible to develop spiritually in unhealthy and unbalanced ways. Finally, without the broader context of the faith tradition and its community, we will eventually run up against our own personal limitations and stop growing. The church provides wisdom, challenge, depth, diversity, support, corrective, historical continuity, and ritual life that simply cannot be found on our own.

At the outset, however, let me be clear about what I mean by Christian community. The modern American parish form is not the only kind of Christian community. In fact, it is entirely possible that whole segments of our population are never likely to feel drawn to parish life

---

1 Quoted by Steindl-Rast, "Recollections of Thomas Merton's Last Days in the West," 1.

because of the parish's tendency to take on cultural qualities that have nothing to do with the faith: dressing up, sitting quietly in rows, listening to and singing particular kinds of music, forming committees, creating and fulfilling ambitious goals, etc. So when I say that Christian community and tradition in some form is essential to every Christian, I recognize that not everyone is going to benefit from the parish as it tends to be in our culture.

There are other models of Christian community where the tradition is celebrated and handed down, which operate under slightly different cultural norms: monasteries, spirituality centers, seminaries, street ministries...far too few, really. But until additional alternatives begin to be more common, the parish as we know it in our culture is the most likely place to find Christian community and its traditions, and quite often, it is a good place to do so.

For a contemplative in particular, remaining grounded in the church and her traditions may present particular difficulties. We can be introverted, individualistic, wary of external forms of religion, and rooted in our own personal experiences. The parish, by its very nature, is more extroverted, institutional, and based upon objective and external forms of authority and teaching.

I cannot count the number of times I have been told that someone is "into spirituality, not organized religion." I am certainly glad that our generation has seized the importance of a personal, meaningful appropriation of faith. I fully understand the serious failings of our institutional church, and I also know how much more deeply some experience God when they are alone in a mountain meadow than when they are in church.

But I am also afraid that we are left with a lot of people who lack the kind of depth, continuity, balance, commitment, and wisdom that comes from an immersion in a faith community and its tradition. Any form of spirituality, if it has any depth, is rooted in and carried forward through history by "organized religion" and its rituals, stories, teachings, and community, even its hierarchy, buildings, and budgets. The institution is what holds together and passes on the spiritual experiences of great numbers of people over a long period of time (as the church has done for the contemplative tradition).

The church offers to the spiritual seeker, to the contemplative, a community of other seekers, who will offer both support and challenge. She offers deeply symbolic, historically grounded rites that express humankind's deepest longings and truths. There are opportunities to serve those in need, time-tested disciplines of spiritual practice, sacred texts, and theological and moral guidance. The church is certainly not perfect. But even her imperfection is of benefit to the spiritual seeker, who must find ways of being spiritual in an imperfect world, and who must also encounter his or her own limitations as they bump up against those of others.

A documentary film called "Monastery" was done many years ago on the Trappist community in Spencer, Massachusetts. One young monk made a comment in an interview that has remained with me ever since I saw it. He said that the monastery "is just like everyday life in the world; the only difference is that we put a frame around it." I believe that the same thing could be said of the church in general.

In local, regional, and worldwide churches, we gather all sorts of people together to engage in all the normal sorts of human activities that we do elsewhere: administration, education, fundraising, social service, community-building, and personal relationships. The only difference is, we put a frame around all of this life. The frame is Jesus Christ and what he called the kingdom of God: love, forgiveness, justice, and worship of our Creator. This is an enormous difference, for it tells us that as the church we are invited to live our everyday lives together in a certain way. Agreeing to this ground rule, we can then set about doing administration, relationships, education, and service to others with a different kind of orientation and goals.

As such, our church life together becomes a microcosm of everyday life, focused in a particular kind of way so that it will serve as a training ground for the rest of life. St. Benedict called the monastery "a school for the Lord's service." For the seeker, life in the church becomes a training school that prepares one for the rest of life.

How can a contemplative, in particular, learn in this school? How can we expand our practice of contemplation so that it is not limited to formal times of prayer, but includes our life in the church? In the pages that follow, I hope to offer some responses to these questions.

Worship

The primary influence on the person who takes part in a vital and healthy church community is the amazingly dense experience of worship. Scripture is read and reflected upon; ceremonial gestures are made; symbols abound; prayers are offered for the world; spiritual lessons are said and sung in the form of psalms, canticles, creeds, and hymns; saints are remembered; history is invoked; community is built; theological themes are celebrated and taught through seasons and festivals; and much more. Liturgical worship is an intense distillation of tradition, through which the church's whole collective historical and contemporary faith is expressed experientially and repetitively.

To be exposed to this week in and week out, season after season, and year after year, one is profoundly influenced. Through story, preaching, poetic expressions of theology, and perhaps most of all through atmosphere, one is led over time into the essence of what it means to be a follower of Jesus Christ. The church's theological perspective on life sinks in. We slowly take in the possibilities of forgiveness, unconditional love, dying to the false self, seeing the sacred in the ordinary, questioning our cultural idols, serving those who suffer, and opening our hearts to one another and God in Christ. Liturgical worship powerfully communicates all of this in an environment that is at once sensory, intellectual, emotional, creative, social, and historical.

For the contemplative, the church's breadth of concern as expressed through the liturgy is just as important as for anyone else, perhaps even more so. In private contemplative practice, one always runs the danger of becoming isolated, overly subjective, and lost in a small personal world of one's own. Liturgical worship offers enough stimulation and challenge to keep contemplatives open to the bigger picture beyond the self alone in relationship to God. It brings in the world, mortality, forgiveness, the hope of new life in resurrection, community, God's judgment of our individual and corporate sin, the call to justice and mercy, the transcendent mystery of God's holiness and the intimacy of the Spirit's loving presence. Left on our own, how many of us would really be able to consistently present ourselves with this breadth of influence?

Baptism is the primary sacrament, the beginning point for a Christian's entrance into life in Christ and the Christian community. Even though it is celebrated only several times a year, it occupies the central place in the life of worship, and therefore carries a potent message. For the contemplative, baptism's message is especially powerful.

There is a mystical, contemplative dimension to baptism that is often overlooked. In fact, it is the same dimension of our faith that is hidden to many Christians, even though it is at the heart of the Christian gospel. I am speaking of the mystical dimension of living in

Christ. While many Christians think that what it means to be a Christian is to do our best to practice virtues and avoid sin (which it is, in part), there is also a deeper call to become Christ.

The life of faith often begins with obligatory do's and don'ts: be kind and forgiving, don't drink too much, do good deeds for those in need, don't get too attached to money, go to church, don't be selfish. But the problem with a faith that is based solely on these injunctions is that we end up trying to be as good as we can, succeeding and failing at this effort, and hoping that somehow in the end we will measure up.

Being a Christian also means, as St. Paul and all the saints after him knew, that we have died to ourselves (that is, what is good or bad about us is ultimately beside the point) and that Christ is risen in us. "It is no longer I who live," said Paul, "but Christ who lives in me." In baptism we do not just celebrate the miracle of birth and our hope that the candidate will be as good as they can. We drown them in the waters of baptism, and we resurrect them to new life in Christ.

In the Christian life, we do not imitate Christ; he lives through us. This is what St. Paul meant by living in Christ, living by faith, living by grace and not by the law. After the baptism by water, the candidates are anointed with oil and thereby "marked as Christ's own forever." Their Christian lives then become a living-out of this new identity. Over time they are transformed by opening to Christ within, and also by coming to self-awareness about all that stands in the way of this opening.

The transformation of life that I describe here is accomplished within the community of faith. All the baptized are joined in this journey together, which is why we celebrate baptism on Sunday mornings, with the whole community gathered. We cannot accomplish dying to self and rising in Christ alone; we need one another's support.

And so for the contemplative, as well as all Christians, baptism is key. It is the visible sign of our true hope, that we will die daily, every time we become aware that we are caught in patterns that alienate us from God, and that we will, again and again, invite Christ to live his life through us. Each time that a baptism is celebrated in the church, we renew our own baptismal covenant together. Much of the language of this rite is about practicing, with God's help, the virtues of the Christian life. But underneath all this language is a profoundly contemplative message about the power of the Paschal Mystery: that in Christ we have died, and he has risen up within us to make himself known through the struggles and delights of our particular lives. He has resurrected into us so that we can die to ourselves and know his life. Further, we come to know this reality together, in the community of the baptized.

Liturgical churches are now in the practice of celebrating the sacrament of eucharist as their weekly form of worship. It is also called the Mass, the Lord's Supper, and Holy Communion. This last name is the most descriptive, really. The word communion points to the whole purpose and mystical nature of the rite: to celebrate and move more deeply into our union with God in Christ and each other. We are in sacred union together: co(mm)union. If the aim of contemplative prayer is union with all in God, there are a number of ways in which the sacrament of Eucharist is an expression of and a means to this union.

The primary form of eucharistic union is with Christ. While in private contemplation we may call upon Jesus' presence through icons or the Jesus Prayer, in communion we are joined with him through his Body and Blood. What could be a more intimate union? Our flesh and blood is mingled with Christ's as we chew and swallow the consecrated bread and wine. Our own lives are given in the offertory of bread and wine, representing our earthy creatureliness, and also in money, representing our time, our life's work. We offer ourselves as we walk up to the altar, opening our heart, ready to give back to God what is God's: our lives. Christ's life is then offered to us, blessed, broken, and distributed to his people. The offering of our lives meets the offering of Christ's life for us at the altar. In this mutual self-giving, we are one. Our lives in Christ are strengthened by our participation in sacramental communion with him.

An important unitive aspect to the sacrament of communion is a joining together of the people of God. In Christ, we are living members of one divine and mystical body. Our separations and distinctions disappear as we hug each other sharing the peace of God, pray for one another, sit together in the pews, and as we stand together at the altar of God. Our body language, our clothing, our whispered prayers, our tears and sighs, our moods and the looks on our faces intimately communicate something about ourselves to others. We know ourselves to be, in these moments, not isolated individual units, as we normally imagine ourselves, but rather one as the Body of Christ.

In Maximus the Confessor's *The Church's Mystagogy*, he articulates what is for many Christians a deeply felt eucharistic experience of mystical communion with one another in Christ; our uniqueness and individuality finding convergence in him during this sacrament. His words are as applicable today in a twenty-first century American parish as they were when he wrote them in a monastery in North Africa in the early seventh century:

> Men, women, children, deeply divided as to race, nationality, language, class, work, knowledge, rank and fortune...everyone is, so to speak, merged into everyone else, by the simple and indivisible power of faith. Christ is thus everything in everyone.[2]

---

2 Quoted by Clement, *The Roots of Christian Mysticism*, 116.

Finally, one of the most powerful forms of contemplative union that communion celebrates is the transcendent, universal prayer of the Church and all creation. The worldwide Church is joined together with saints, angels, and all the creatures of God who raise their voices in praise, singing "Holy, Holy, Holy Lord, God of power and might, heaven and earth are full of your glory: hosanna in the highest!" It is indeed "a foretaste of the heavenly banquet."

For the contemplative, this is nothing less than the complete fulfillment of what is experienced privately in prayer: the union of human and divine, earth and heaven, past and future, life and death, time and eternity, what is seen and what is unseen, known and unknown. The union that is found in contemplative solitude is exploded outwards infinitely in communion, to include all of the creatures of God in the adoration of their Creator.

Regular participation in eucharistic worship is not only good for the contemplative; it is an essential part of a specifically Christian contemplative life, where we join ourselves sacramentally with Christ, with one another, and with all creation in mystic union.

The Practice of Community

The parish offers a kind of community that is rare in our society today. Like some small towns that provide intimate proximity between neighbors, friends, adversaries, and generations of relatives and in-laws, everyone in the parish belongs and is accepted. Where else these days can we experience what it is like to be part of an extended family? Where else can we test out our faith in relationship with those we like, those we do not like, and those we barely know, but all of whom we are connected with over time?

While some people in community inevitably come and go like the weather, most stay around awhile. A relatively stable population meets regularly, opening their hearts together in worship, struggling over budgets and plans, and wrestling with the mysteries of the faith. Over the years, they come to know one another somewhat intimately as they reveal who they are to one another.

In the parish community, we may be constantly rubbing elbows with people that we would not normally choose as friends. Serving together on committees, sitting in the pews together, talking over coffee or a potluck dinner, studying in a class, we encounter one another. Because we are dealing with issues of faith, personal transformation, and serving those who suffer, we meet one another in depth, at least potentially. We do not get to pick out who we will encounter in these depths. We work with whomever is put in our path.

Most of those people are delightful, and not much needs to be said about the benefit of working with them. We enjoy what they offer us, as they expand our horizons and teach us to see things in a new way. This is one of the real joys of community life.

There are also always a few difficult members of the parish. They are also our teachers. Those who are emotionally unhealthy or irritating force us to take seriously the teachings of Christ. Through them we learn how to love unconditionally, and also how to stand firm and set needed boundaries with kindness. They push our buttons, and thereby reveal to us uncomfortable truths about ourselves. Others are difficult for us because they think differently about the faith than we do; they force us to become clearer about what we believe, and teach us the value and possibility of living respectfully with our differences.

There is a story about the spiritual teacher Gurdjieff, whose community suffered long with a particularly obnoxious member and eventually pressured him to leave. It is said that Gurdjieff chased after him until he found him in a nearby town, begging him to return because of the way the community kept learning from his presence.

When relationships are hard in the parish community, the contemplative can bring dedicated awareness to the situation. Choosing to practice with the relationship rather than ignoring, reacting, resisting, or running away from it, the contemplative can hold the other in prayerful awareness. Awareness reveals to us our own anger, attraction, distrust, arrogance, compassion, or whatever else is really there. Coming to the point of reality, we are then finally able to offer the relationship to God as it is, and surrender to grace, that we may be renewed in faith, love, and truth. This renewal might take the form of an honest confrontation, an action, or acceptance and letting-go. But whatever form it takes, if it is rooted in contemplative prayer and self-awareness, it will be influenced by greater clarity, humility, and love.

The church is not perfect, but like the "good enough" parent, a phrase coined by the child psychoanalyst Donald Winnicott, often the parish community is good and healthy enough. Often it does provide enough of the breadth of our tradition, an experience of sacramental union, the foundation of scripture, study of the faith, healthy authority and other relationships, and opportunity to serve social needs.

Being "good enough," it is important that we remain in one place instead of casting about seeking perfection. Staying put, we learn from the depth and difficulty of ourselves in relation to others, rather than running away from things when they get difficult, only to find, of course, that the same problem exists everywhere we go. The sixth century father of western monasticism, Benedict of Nursia, enshrined this principle within the structure of Benedictine spirituality by making *stability* to be one of the three vows taken by the monk or nun, by which he or she promises to remain in one community for the rest of his or her life.

Benedict was profoundly influenced by the earlier desert fathers and mothers, and one of them, Amma Syncletia, expresses the spiritual value of stability quite clearly:

> If you find yourself in a monastery do not go to another place, for that will harm you a great deal. Just as the bird who abandons the eggs she was sitting on prevents them from hatching, so the monk or the nun grows cold and their faith dies, when they go from one place to another.[3]

Perhaps Amma Syncletia's "eggs" are those lessons borne from difficulty from which we can potentially learn. How many times have we seen those whose faith never "hatches," in part because they have left the eggs they were sitting on in another parish community, preferring the illusion of a "geographical cure" instead? While it is certain that sometimes we must leave a community, when it becomes destructive and we are not able to help by our efforts, all too often we leave too easily, exercising our cultural tendency to seek out a new church as if it were a commodity, obtained or discarded by the criterion of whether or not it is "meeting our needs." Forever moving along, the spiritual wanderers never hatch the "eggs" of struggle that will develop anywhere, if they stick around long enough. The contemplative path calls us to stay put, to reflect deeply on what we need to learn from any given difficulty, rather than trying to discard it because it is uncomfortable.

The women elders of the early desert tradition seemed to understand this principle. Perhaps this has something

---

3 *The Sayings of the Desert Fathers*, Ward, 231.

to do with women's traditional role in holding a family together emotionally, spiritually, no matter what struggles arise. In a strikingly similar saying, another desert mother, Amma Theodora, taught her disciples that one could never get away from oneself, especially by trying to make external changes. The second "man" in the story is the monk's own temptations:

> There was a monk, who, because of the great number of his temptations said, "I will go away from here." As he was putting on his sandals, he saw another man who was also putting on his sandals and this other monk said to him, "Is it on my account that you are going away? Because I go before you wherever you are going."[4]

Ordinary Parish Work

Another element of parish community that provides ample opportunity for spiritual practice is in the ordinary, everyday work that is involved in running the business and organizations of a parish. Rather than being a "distraction" from more spiritual matters, the everyday work of parish life can be seen as an opportunity to incarnate the faith in the realities of living in the world.

Whether we are hammering out drastic cuts in a budget, making sure the church is clean for Sunday services, dealing with the details of who is going to make coffee, or pondering the problems of the office computers, each moment brings the contemplative an opportunity to be faithful. How we engage with all these concerns tells us a great deal about ourselves. Do we do it with anxiety, afraid that we'll come across as incompetent? Do we do it with impatience and frustration, just trying to get the damn thing done?

---

4 *Ibid.*, 84.

Do we do it with a sense of perspective and humor, knowing that it really is not all that important in the light of eternity? Do we look for wonder in this moment of creation, can we see the sacred in this specific set of circumstances?

Contemplative practice must take everything into account, each moment and detail, and it must seek God's presence in the ordinary. Otherwise it runs the danger of serving the illusion of "special moments" with God, boxed into little preconceived, stereotyped forms. The ordinariness of parish life is an integral part of spiritual practice. By taking its details seriously as avenues into divinity, we can take them lightly also. For it is not so much what we do, when we get it done, how well organized we are, how much money we save or make, or how perfect or faulty our parish is that matters. Rather, what is important is how we do what we do. By paying close attention to how we work with the ordinary, its outcome becomes paradoxically less important. Such a perspective could be called engaged detachment. As Joko Beck's own Zen teacher once said to her, "Nothing matters!…Everything matters!" And as T.S. Eliot wrote in his poem 'Ash Wednesday,' "Lord, teach us to care and not to care."

Serving Others

If we spend time in a parish we cannot go for long (I hope) without being invited to take part in some kind of service to people in need. Parish programs point us towards hospital, prison or nursing home visitations, building homes for low-income families, donating food, mentoring youngsters at risk, advocating local and global policies that are economic, ecological, or educational in nature, and many other activities. The church invites us both to serve those in need and to work for social change.

Long ago in the medieval West, there developed a division between those who were "called to the contemplative life" and those who were "called to the active life." Religious orders designated themselves one or the other, and Christians saw them as two separate activities. We still live with this legacy.

It is true that God endows some people with a more natural inclination and gifts for some activities and less for others. We cannot all be activists, and we cannot all be mystics. Nor should we try to be. But in this division between callings, we have also given the message that somehow either prayer or service is not necessary for some Christians. I do not believe this is true. Prayer is the way in which all of God's children can reach out in relationship to their Creator; service is a natural responsibility that comes from our belonging to one another in the Spirit. Contemplatives are not exempt from service to and advocacy for those in need.

Those who are service-oriented have, in the story of Martha and Mary, a cautionary tale about getting so wrapped up in worthwhile activity that they forget to stay connected to the One who calls them to this activity. Contemplatives have this warning about worship and prayer that does not result in justice and care for those in need:

> I cannot endure solemn assemblies with iniquity…your new moons and your appointed festival my soul hates; they have become a burden to me, I am weary of bearing them. When you stretch out your hands, I will hide my eyes from you; even though you make many prayers, I will not listen…learn to do good; seek justice, rescue the oppressed, defend the orphan, plead for the widow (Is.1:13b–15a, 17).

Clearly our tradition teaches us that we are all called to love, to be compassionate, and to be pro-active about addressing the needs of the world. Some do this as a natural inclination, some do so because they know they should, and others find themselves more actively compassionate because their hearts have been transformed through prayer.

The whole purpose of any spiritual discipline, including contemplative prayer, is to be transformed so that we might then serve, love, liberate, and transform the world around us. In the end, we engage in prayer and meditation so that we might be instruments of God's grace and healing for others. Without this purpose what is the point of personal transformation? To feel holy?

The healthy parish community offers a number of ways that we can take part in service to others. For the contemplative, these ministries, as well as opportunities to serve outside the parish, offer a way to incarnate the divine union we experience in prayer. In contemplation, we come to know that we are one with God, one with Christ, one with each other, and one with all creation. If this is really experienced in an integrative way, it will find its natural expression in our actions. Because we are one, we will not be able to help ourselves; we will just serve.

Serving others, if it is to be helpful, must be selfless. And for service to be another way of practicing prayer in action, as a contemplative we must learn to recognize the various ways in which we seek benefit or advantage through our serving. Through this self-awareness, we can learn to give more selflessly.

Some of us discover that we serve, in part, because we want to be appreciated and liked. Others serve because it makes us feel superior to those who are served. Others do so out of guilt and duty. Some of us serve only those whom we think will appreciate our efforts, who are "truly needy and deserving" and will not take advantage of our largesse, or who will give back to us and others as a result of our serving them.

But true service is empty of all these motivations. True service is an act of loving compassion that has no reason, no justification, no payback, or deserving. True service helps those in need because they need the help. Period. This is, like almsgiving, an essentially contemplative stance born out of self-emptying. It is a free gift that comes naturally when we bring self-awareness to our motivations that are born out of attachments and ambitions, and lay them before God in humility.

But it is not about not having self-serving motivations—we all do, because we are human—rather, it is about ringing awareness to the ones we do have. When we bring awareness to our motivations, we are then in a better position to be freer from them than we would be without having done so. We then serve simply because service is needed.

In the parish, generous people devise creative ways of responding to pain and need through various ministries. The contemplative, joining together with others in these ministries, finds that this kind of activity is nothing less than a self-emptying response to our union in God with one another. Sitting in contemplative silence, we are given a taste of what is real: that we are all held together in God's life. There is no separation between any of us. There is no separation between the one who prays and the ones who are prayed for. The social service dimension of the church is one place where this reality of union may be incarnated in a powerful way.

The Contemplative's Gift to the Church

Up to this point, I have focused on ways in which the church may provide support, challenge, and spiritual practice for the contemplative Christian. But there are very real and important ways in which the contemplative brings great benefit to the church as well.

In my parish, I am frequently told how important the presence of our Contemplative Center[5] is to our overall parish life. This is expressed not only by those who attend its programs, but also by others who may never do so. What they say is that the presence of people who devote themselves to deep prayer has a powerful effect upon the parish. They can sense that they are surrounded, here and there, by people who are really devoted to God, who pray every day. There is an impact from these people's presence in the common liturgy, in the education classes, in committees, and in coffee hour conversation. What is this impact?

It is the presence of the Spirit, felt unmistakably by anyone with a sensitivity to such things. Contemplatives who spend a part of each day seriously opening themselves to the Spirit of God cannot help but give off something of their contact with the divine. I do not mean to be dramatic about it, as if "special" people are walking around with golden auras. I just mean that there is something evident about a person's sustained contact with the Spirit: calm, a comfort with silence, a quiet joy, a lack of anxiety, a confidence in being. If a group of just five or ten such people regularly attend worship with the rest of the community, their presence will be felt in worship.

Years ago, Martin Thornton wrote a wonderful book, *The Heart of the Parish: a Theology of the Remnant* (Cambridge: Cowley Publications, 1989), in which he argues that the center of parish life is the faith development of the "faithful remnant," those few people

---

5 The Contemplative Center offers contemplative prayer groups, retreats, quiet days, conferences, and spiritual formation through a Rule of Life for its participants, who come from within and beyond the parish. See chapter 6, "Finding Support," for more information.

who are committed to spiritual growth through a life of prayer. In fact, Thornton suggests that clergy should devote a proportionally higher amount of time to assisting with their formation, a lesser amount to those who are "willing but undisciplined," and even less to the "multitudes." This is the exact opposite of the church growth movement, which often is more about numbers than faithfulness.

Thornton bases his argument upon Jesus' own model of how he spent his time in ministry. The reason for this emphasis is to build up the core, the heart of what the local community of faith is all about, so that everyone may benefit. When the parish is spiritually vital at the center, including, most importantly, the clergy, the parish is vital. When the clergy and laity at the heart of things are not spiritually alive and healthy, the parish lies dormant, even lifeless, or co-opted by cultural values, or worse, becomes destructive.

All the service and worship and business of parish life is either an expression of God's loving presence or it is simply activity. The profound difference between the two is rooted in the hearts of those at the center who pray or who do not pray. Clergy and lay leaders who devote themselves to a life of prayer will communicate, by their very being, the love, vitality, and peace of God through their worship, teaching, preaching, pastoral care, casual conversations and everything else they do. They will be a living witness to what they talk about and celebrate through the varying forms of church life.

In my experience these people carry an inner authority with them that then influences how the community functions. Others watch how they act, and if it is centered in God, they follow. Therefore, prayerful people who patiently listen to God regularly will help the community to do the same when it comes to discerning direction for parish life, instead of leaping ahead into hastily-crafted goals and objectives, as if it were just a business. People who practice careful self-awareness will be less likely to be reactive in their relationships, and this helps others to do the same. People who know that God is the most important reality in their lives will help the community to risk following what they believe to be God's will for the parish instead of relying upon conventional wisdom and common sense alone.

I am not saying that people who practice contemplative prayer are better or are the only ones in parish life who can offer this kind of example. Any person of faith will do the same. But faith comes through a life of some kind of prayer. In prayer we meet and are transformed by the living God. There are always those in every parish who know this prayerful transformation, and contemplatives can be some of them.

Historically, the contemplative tradition has also served the rest of the church as a witness to a certain theological perspective. It has held up the possibility of, even the confidence in, our ability to realize our union with God. It has refused simplistic theological certainties offered by many others in the church, preferring instead to live with paradox, mystery, and unknowing. It has emphasized a living encounter with the Holy One when others have stressed beliefs, moral obedience, and external forms. It has held out a radical vision of dying to the very notion of a self, entering in faith to the darkness of no self, and finding in that very place our true life in God.

In the local contemporary parish, the contemplative may not feel that they are really providing much witness to these things. But they are, simply by their willingness to sit in silence and wait for God. They witness to these themes by their participation, however small, in the ongoing stream of the contemplative tradition in the church. Through their participation in this stream, they ensure that it will keep on flowing to the next generation of seekers. A contemplative prayer group might not ever attract more than a few participants. But even these few people can serve as a subtle reminder of divine union, mystery, real engagement with God, and dying to self.

There is also another aspect to the presence of contemplatives in a parish that has to do with just being, for others, ones who pray. Parishioners who know that individuals or a group of people devote themselves to indepth prayer are somehow comforted and strengthened by that knowledge. Years ago the Grubb Institute in England did a survey of people to find out what significance the Church of England had for them personally. Even in towns where attendance on Sundays was abysmally low, in most towns, actually, people would often comment that while they did not attend church, they felt it was important that the church was there, and that some people did attend.

We can laugh at this sentiment, but there is something to it. Some have considered regular members of the parish to be "keepers of the shrine," or those who keep the lamp of Christ lit. Whatever else they do, perhaps one of the key things is their willingness to keep the doors open and the gospel proclaimed. People who never attend church worship can benefit from the awareness that somehow they are linked to others who worship; the others' prayers are appreciated, even felt.

The same is true for the contemplative and other prayerful people in the parish. Many in parish life never pray outside of public worship, or they do so only in short bursts during moments of need. But the knowledge that there are some in their community of faith who are keeping the flame lit, the door open, comforts and strengthens them spiritually. That is because, again, we are connected in Christ as one Body. In the same sense, a more spirituality-oriented person is helped by the knowledge and presence of others in the community who devote themselves to helping people in need.

We cannot all be Mother Theresa of Calcutta and we cannot all be Thomas Merton. Not all have the gift of compassionate service to the helpless and not all are called to contemplative prayer. But we can be ourselves, and we can strengthen one another in the Body of Christ by the offering of our various gifts. The gift of the contemplative is prayer, and their prayer is not for themselves alone, but for everyone.

In this sense the prayer of the contemplative is not a private affair. Even when they are not engaged in intercessory prayer, their prayer is linked with all others in Christ's Body, because we are all one. The prayer of one becomes the prayer of all. The devotion of one person's prayer helps another person's faith. While we modern Westerners tend to think individually, the more ancient and Jewish understanding of faith is that it is a corporate thing. It was the faithfulness of the people of Israel that mattered. Perhaps we can return to this understanding in Christian community, and celebrate the various gifts we can offer one another, so that the faith of the community will be built up over time. St. Paul said:

> In Christ the whole structure [of the household of God] is joined together and grows into a holy temple in the Lord; in whom you are also built together spiritually into a dwelling place for God (Eph.3:21–22).

Contemplatives have a significant role to play in the building up of the household of God. Through their witness to a certain theological perspective, their inner authority, their groundedness in the Spirit, and their whole way of being, they participate in helping the community become "a holy temple of the Lord." They help it become what it truly is, the body of Christ.

Five

❈

Traditional Disciplines

THE LAST CHAPTER ENCOURAGED the contemplative to enter prayerfully into the life of the local parish, so that personal contemplative practice can be balanced, integrated, and broadened. As such the themes were general: worship, community, church work, service. If one enters into the church's life even further, certain specific highlights may start to become visible, at least to the discerning eye: the traditional spiritual disciplines of the church. These disciplines include, among other things, the Daily Office, intercessory prayer, almsgiving, self-denial, confession, and studying the faith tradition.

In order to grow in our faith, we must undergo training that has been shaped by the spiritual experts of the ages, and not limit ourselves to personalized prayer alone. To do the latter would be as if a musician endeavored to become a mature artist and stuck to playing only his own compositions, never practicing scales, arpeggios, etudes, and works of the masters. Similarly, if we want to progress in the kind of life that is set forth by the luminaries who speak of Christian spiritual freedom and love, we must do what they did. We must practice the traditional disciplines that they utilized, in the hopes that as we make them our own, they will also bear fruit in our lives.

To do so, it is critical that we understand and practice these disciplines in a way that makes sense to us, that fits into the demands of a busy modern life, and that originates from a loving desire for God, not from rigid duty. The traditional disciplines of the church are a gift from the saints, a gift that helps us open our hearts to God in creative and challenging ways. The purpose of these disciplines is to help us make ourselves more and more available to our loving God. Instead of practicing them with determined, self-punishing seriousness, we use them as various paths upon which we invite the Spirit into all the corners of our lives.

Like any form of discipline, these practices should be undertaken gradually, not all at once. No sane athlete sits down and decides that today she is going to start eating all the right food, swimming each morning, bicycling to work, lifting weights in the evening, and running marathons on the weekends. No person of faith should do the same. Over a lifetime, we patiently re-orient our lifestyles. Gradually we incorporate new practices that attract and make sense to us, and utilize them when and how we can. They are presented here in one continuous flow because this is a book. But in life, we find them here and there; we undertake one of them, drop it, and return to it later with a fresh perspective. What is important is that over time, we keep returning to the possibility that these disciplines may have something to teach us by their use.

For the contemplative, they are important because they stretch us beyond our personal limitations, into the depths of the church's wisdom. As I hope to show, these disciplines also contain within each of them what I believe to be a contemplative dimension.

The Daily Office

A once-a-week Sunday immersion in the faith community, her sacred texts and her liturgy keeps a contemplative basically rooted in the church's tradition and teaching. The Anglican tradition offers a way of staying connected on a daily basis as well.

Thomas Cranmer, the great architect of our first *Book of Common Prayer* (1549), borrowed many prayers and rites from ancient sources. One of his strongest influences was the Benedictine monastic life, which prior to the Reformation, dominated England more than it did any other nation in Europe. This influence included, in particular, Benedictine monastic communities in British cathedrals and their abbey schools. It would not be an exaggeration to say that England's religious character, even its culture, to some extent, is imbued with a Benedictine flavor. The nature of this flavor is an emphasis on the ordinary dimensions of life as the primary place of encounter with God: a belief that moderation is essential to a healthy religious life; a balance of prayer, study, and work; and a regular rhythm of sober and straightforward worship that is rooted in the psalms, scripture, and prayers for the church and the world.

Cranmer looked to this familiar Benedictine way of being Christian as one of the foundations for the Prayer Book, which ordered the church's private prayer and public worship. From the start, Anglicans were expected to keep the Benedictine-style round of daily prayers, either privately or in their churches. Only instead of the daily eight times of structured prayers or offices of the late medieval monastery, Cranmer put forth consolidated, simplified forms for Morning and Evening Prayer. The contemporary Episcopal *Book of Common Prayer* offers four full offices, and several shorter options as well.[1] Many Anglicans have been shaped by a

---

1 *The Book of Common Prayer* provides instruction for the recitation of each office in the form of rubrics, those italicized directives found throughout. In addition, assigned psalms and readings from scripture are listed beginning on page 934 of the BCP. If you are unfamiliar with the use of these resources, it is best to get some help and advice from a clergy or lay person who knows how to use them.

commitment to this central discipline ever since, praying in the morning as the day begins, and in the evening as it ends.

Most contemplatives whose writings or names have survived historically, whether Roman, Anglican, or Orthodox, are monks. They practice the discipline of daily offices, or the Liturgy of the Hours. While these forms of prayer may not be what we call "contemplative" in themselves, they are an important, central part of the contemplative's prayer life. And so for contemplative monastics and Anglican clergy and many laity, the Daily Office is key.

The office is basically an immersion in scripture from beginning to end. Opening sentences from the Bible begin the office, psalms are said or chanted, canticles (biblical poems or songs of worship) are alternated with readings from scripture, and one reads written prayers that are basically re-worded phrases from the Bible. When you do Morning and/or Evening Prayer on a daily basis over some time, you cycle through all of the psalms and most of Holy Scripture. The assigned readings include one from the Hebrew scriptures, one from the Gospels, and one from the remainder of the New Testament. This daily and comprehensive exposure to scripture keeps us rooted in the inspiration and truth of God's Word.

For some, the daily exposure to assigned readings and psalms takes some getting used to. First of all, the readings are relatively short. If you only do the offices once in awhile, you will only be exposed to passages out of context, and it will probably seem disconnected. But if you do them daily, you will find that they usually follow in course, so that today's readings are a contin-uation of yesterday's. Secondly, many of the psalms and some of the readings can be pretty angry, judgmental, or otherwise not the kind of thing most of us would prefer to be reflecting upon prayerfully.

I do not have an easy answer to this latter problem. Some people sort of psychologize the readings, seeing Israel's "enemies" to be squashed by God as one's own sin or unhealthy tendencies. Others try to look at it all in terms of historical context, accepting the fact that whether we like it or not, the authors of scripture in their day were influenced by cultural norms that are no longer held, and they therefore sometimes believed and wrote things about God that we would not. In one way or another, most people who stick with it, including contemplatives, somehow make their peace with the "difficult" psalms and readings.

I just read them, and whether I agree with them or not does not seem to matter much. They are expressions of real human emotions and beliefs, written in the sincere desire to seek and communicate about God. Scripture is a vast collection of differing points of view, and it is not internally consistent throughout. Vengeance and unconditional forgiveness are expressed side by side, and that does not make the whole thing invalid. I do not have to take offense at something I think is spiritually off-base, for who am I to judge these things? I just read them, give thanks for whatever speaks to me in the moment, which sometimes includes some of the angry psalms, and let go of the rest. God works through it all.

I would hate to think what would result if I, like Thomas Jefferson, took scissors to all the passages of scripture I disagreed with or was offended by or thought were "untrue" about God. My edited version of the Bible would end up being just about as small and as limited as I am. I would rather read and pray my way through the whole thing, warts and all.

In addition to an immersion in scripture, the Daily Office leads us in a balanced way through everything the church wants us to experience: seasonal thematic emphases (light in Christmas and Epiphany, penitence in Lent, joyful new life in Easter, and so on), confession of our sins, the Lord's Prayer, intercession for the church, the poor, and all who suffer, and an appeal for God's grace to be faithful this day.

The offices are written in the voice of the church. Their prayers are in a formal style. Some balk at praying to God in this formal voice, and feel that when they read such prayers, they are not really praying, because it is not spontaneous and personal. Private prayer in the form of liturgical language is not for everyone. But for others, it is of great benefit, and as they come to know these prayers by heart, they do become spontaneous and personal. One of my favorite heart-felt prayers is this:

> Heavenly Father, in you we live and move and have our being. We humbly pray you so to guide and govern us by your Holy Spirit, that in all the cares and occupations of our life we may not forget you, but may remember that we are ever walking in your sight.[2]

The language of prayer in the offices is consistently plural. Praying with *The Book of Common Prayer* is almost always "we," not "I." This is critical, especially for the private contemplative. In the office we join our voice of prayer with the whole voice of the church, women and men everywhere who pray to God as one. When we sit alone and recite an office, we do so with others who are praying at the same time and in the same words. Together we offer our common concerns to our common Creator, on behalf of one another and of the whole world.

This helps us especially when it seems impossible for us to pray well, or to pray at all. There are many times, including when I am ill, over-stressed, or going through emotional difficulty, when I just cannot sit silently and effectively open to God. It is in these times that I can say

---

2 *The Book of Common Prayer*, p. 100.

the Daily Office without worrying too much about how I am doing in prayer; for after all, in the office the church is praying through me. I can let the prayer of the church carry me to God when I have no strength to carry myself.

The use of the church's voice in private prayer also teaches us by its use. Over time the theology of the Church seeps through these familiar prayers into our souls. We pray the Incarnation, the Passion, the Resurrection, the grace of the Spirit; all the orthodox faith is expressed through the prayers of the office. Because in prayer our hearts are open in a special way, this affects us. Through the formal written prayers of the Prayer Book, the truth of the gospel and the theology of the church shape our faith on a daily basis.

It is, however, the psalms that form what might be the core of the office, especially for the contemplative. For millennia, Jews and Christians of both East and West have opened their hearts to God through this remarkable poetry of prayer. The psalms contain every human emotion: rage, wonder, love, terror, hope, paranoia, adoration, emptiness, joy, revenge, despair, and hope. Even if we are not feeling the sentiment that one of the assigned psalms for the day is expressing, over time we feel it all.

There is something about the regular recitation of psalms in their totality that leads us into the self-offering of all of life to God. While this will not come across with an occasional use of the psalms, in the long term their voices begin to become our own voice; we honestly lift every part of our lives, whether noble or ugly, to God in this remarkable poetry. With regular use, when we open the Psalter and start to read, we drop into a place where our hearts open with the deepest truth of our lives, where we are able to just be ourselves before God, where an honest relationship with the One who loves us and guides us is sustained in an intimate conversation.

Because the psalms are used so universally in prayer, especially by contemplatives, their recitation also leads us into a sense of praying with everyone else through all time. We sit in our homes or in our churches praying the psalms with not only other Anglicans, Romans, and Orthodox, but all Christians who use them, all monastics, saints of centuries past, and the desert mystics who penned them.

I believe that the use of the Daily Office is helpful for the contemplative for several reasons. First, it keeps us grounded in a daily rhythm of prayer, and every morning and evening if we use two of them, immersed in the inspiration, challenge, and objective truth of scripture, as well as in the breadth of the church's concerns for prayer. The corporate, plural nature of the office's language also helps move us out of isolation, linking us to the prayers of and for the whole church.

In addition, the offices provide a healthy springboard for contemplation (see the section on *Lectio divina* in chapter 3). If we do more than one office a day, they can inspire us to more than one daily period of contemplative prayer, as it flows naturally, even for a few minutes, after the recitation of each office.

Finally, through the beautiful and historic language of the psalms and prayers, we are lifted up by the church into a more holy and orthodox expression of our inner lives. This is important for contemplatives, as it is for anyone, because over time our faith is shaped by this language.

Intercessory Prayer

As contemplatives, none of us is just a solitary being who seeks individual union with God. We are in relationship with friends, strangers, fellow parishioners, neighbors, those who have died, people at work, and vast numbers of others whom we will never know personally but with whom we are nonetheless linked. All these people suffer from time to time, they hunger for God, they are trying to figure out how to go forward in their lives, and they have other very real needs. When one spends time in the parish community and her life of worship, all of this becomes obvious and evident over time. Contemplatives find themselves called not only to the empty, open, and agenda-free quality of silent prayer, they also become drawn into intercessory prayer through their lives in community.

When we pray for others, contemplatives often leave behind the more silent forms of prayer and do so with words, in liturgical forms, and by asking specifically for certain outcomes. This can be a good way for us to balance our prayer lives, but it is also possible to do intercessory prayer in a particularly contemplative way.

Intercessory prayer is a way of realizing and acting upon our spiritual union with others. It is a way of opening our hearts and expressing loving-kindness to all who are in need. To intercede for another means that in our prayer we stand between—or next to—them and God. We lovingly accompany the other in her or his need. This is, really, a contemplative stance, since it requires of us presence more than action. In intercession, we simply hold the other as an offering, asking God to do whatever is needed for her or his benefit.

In contemplative intercession, instead of asking God what we think should be done for others, we simply hold them in our hearts before the One who knows their need before we ask. So rather than being specific in our request—"please heal Mary....bring peace and justice to Jews and Palestinians...help Frank find a new job..."—we might just bring them to mind in prayer, and without words, remain awhile in communion with them and God, feeling their need and our desire for whatever is best for them.

This more contemplative approach to intercession can also be applied to the times when we pray for our own need, by just holding, feeling, knowing the need we have and remaining present with that before God, the source of all good. Gerhart Tersteegen, an eighteenth-century German Protestant contemplative and lay preacher, spoke of this kind of sustained and open-hearted prayer, which can be for our own needs or the needs of another:

> We must just say simply and briefly what we are and what we would like to be; yes, it is not even necessary always to say it, we should just allow God, the ever-present, all-loving one to see us thus—but not perfunctorily: we should try to keep close in front of him for some time, that he may have a good look at us and cure us. We must tell him nothing and let him see nothing but what is in us, whatever it may be.[3]

In praying this way for others, we are acknowledging our basic connectedness with others in God, and counting on that communion to affect some good. When we open up the channels of communion between ourselves, others, and God, something shifts, I believe, and we enable the Spirit to flow more freely where it is needed. It is not that in intercession we convince God to do something that God wouldn't otherwise do; it is that we are all profoundly connected in the Spirit, and by opening doors to that connection, our participation and desire adds something to the communion that was not there before. Healing, peace, freedom, insight, or whatever else is needed becomes more possible because we have done our part in removing obstacles to their emerging.

---

3 Gerhart Tersteegen, *The Quiet Way*, trans. Emily Chisholm (New York: Philosophical Library) 23.

Intercession needn't be limited to praying for other people's needs. We also pray for all of God's creation. The seventh-century monk Isaac of Syria draws no limit to prayer, no line beyond which our love must reach; when he was asked, "what is a compassionate heart?" he responded:

> It is a heart that burns with love for the whole of creation—for men and women, for the birds, for the beasts, for the demons, for every creature...Therefore he never ceases to pray, with tears even for the irrational animals, for the enemies of truth, and for those who do him evil, asking that they may be guarded and receive God's mercy. And for the reptiles also he prays with a great compassion which rises up endlessly in his heart until he shines again and is glorious like God.[4]
> ~ *Ascetic Treatises*, 81

So contemplative prayer can include an intercessory, petitionary intention, and in this way, the contemplative responds more broadly to the church's call to pray for all people everywhere in their various needs, and even for the whole of creation.

Giving Money

Parishioners often hear about the church's need for money, and are invited to pledge to the operating fund and other purposes. Giving money is an integral part of being a member in a parish, and I believe that it also presents an important opportunity for contemplative practice that is often overlooked.

Giving money is traditionally called almsgiving when referred to as a spiritual discipline. An ancient and

---

4 Quoted by Clement, *The Roots of Christian Mysticism*, 227.

annual tradition of the church at the beginning of the season of Lent is the call to the faithful to practice in a more dedicated way the three-fold discipline of prayer, fasting, and almsgiving. Almsgiving is the intentional, free release of a portion of our resources through pledging to our parishes, donating to charitable causes, handing someone on the street a dollar or taking them to a diner for a sandwich, giving money to a friend or family member in need, or any other form of financial giving with no strings attached.

This is done as a spiritual discipline for many reasons. Since we are created in God's image, and are at our best when we are faithful to that image, and since God is generous, we too are at our most loving and free when we are generous. We probably all know someone who is a model of this kind of generosity, and we know how happy it makes them and everyone around them.

But almsgiving is also a spiritual discipline because through it we break down our attachment to security and self-centeredness. To give away money is a direct, frontal assault on a primary kind of attachment. Many will avoid it, saying that there are other, better, more "spiritual" ways of being generous and serving others, so leave my money out of it! Money is powerful, giving us the illusion of complete control, and with it we can form a serious, idolatrous attachment. This is why the biblical warning that "the love of money is a root of all kinds of evil" (1 Tim.6:10), while a bit of an overstatement, has such truth to it. Note that it is the *love* of money, our attachment to it, that causes the problem rather than money itself, which is neutral and can be used for good or for ill.

To commit to giving away a percentage of our financial income is a way to break that attachment, because it forces us to commit to a regular, systematic discipline that puts our priorities into action. Instead of giving just when we feel moved to do so and in an amount that seems to make sense at the time, proportional giving is a spiritual discipline, like prayer, that keeps us moving in a direction that we know we need to go, come rain or shine.

Almsgiving is also a way of practicing, in a concrete way, that contemplative task of self-emptying. In emptying ourselves through prayer, we create space that the Spirit can fill. In emptying ourselves of some measure of our security, self-indulgence and attachment to money, we create space, again, where the Spirit can move more freely. Through almsgiving we empty ourselves of a powerful form of control and security, releasing it out to others, so that our attachment is transformed into many blessings for other people. Its energy is thereby transformed from something that can be destructive to something that is holy. In the process, we too are blessed, for as Jesus taught us again and again, it is in dying to self that we are born into eternal life.

Self-denial

Another traditional Lenten discipline is fasting. I remember growing up in an Episcopal family when, as a part of this season, we all "gave up" something for Lent. I always gave up chocolate. I still love dark chocolate, and I suppose that when as a twelve year-old I gave it up for Lent there was really some kind of disciplined self-sacrifice going on in my soul. My mother always gave me a giant See's chocolate egg for Easter. She still does, and it often arrives on Good Friday, appearing as a kind of perverse maternal temptation for me to forsake my penitence on that day. I usually give in.

While "giving up something for Lent" has its benefits, the discipline of self-denial and fasting can be much broader and more lasting in its impact. The purpose of this practice is to create an empty space that would otherwise be filled by something habitual, in order to make some room where God can be experienced in a new way.

We all have habits that serve to comfort, distract, and entertain ourselves. There is often nothing wrong with them. These habits can be a way of creating a consoling sense of order and being good to ourselves; they can be a part of enjoying all the wonderful things that life has to offer. We come home tired, open a beer and flip on the television and feel relieved that nothing, not even thinking, will be required of us. We create a delicious meal and share it with friends; we buy a new colorful shirt; or we indulge ourselves in celebrity, sports, or fashion magazines.

But there are also times when it is helpful to examine our habits, in order to see how we use some of them in ways that are ultimately not life-giving. Some of those habits may give us temporary order, relief, or pleasure, but in the long run they may also bring us disorder, attachment, emptiness, and dispersion of spirit. Sometimes we do not know what to do with ourselves if we do not shop, eat, drink, watch TV, or talk.

Self-denial is a way of addressing this problem. To deny ourselves, for a period of time, one of our habitual comforts, attachments, or distractions, we create an empty space. We stop eating snacks and limit ourselves to one small serving per meal; or we refrain from alcohol; we turn off the television, radio, and computer; we decide to stop gossiping; we avoid errands and stay home one day a week; or we undertake a juice-only fast and keep silence for twenty-four hours. Any of these forms of self-denial creates an empty space that we are otherwise accustomed to filling.

When we withdraw the act of filling, we discover something uncomfortable about ourselves. We discover the sense of loneliness that we are trying to console with food or alcohol, or we discover the feeling of being lost that we cover with incessant activity. To fast from anything that is habitual is to withdraw a means of support, and the result is discomfort. Hunger is uncomfortable, and so is silence, inactivity, or a lack of stimulation. In our world that is so saturated by media, product, activity, and information, self-denial is not only difficuly, it is counter-cultural. It is hard to see why anyone would do such a thing. We are so conditioned towards self-fulfillment that it does not occur to most of us why we should deliberately make ourselves uncomfortable.

But our Christian tradition teaches us that in the discomfort there are great rewards. As we encounter our emptiness, our loneliness and need, we open the gate that leads to God. In our emptiness we are less likely to be cluttered by lots of things that normally obscure the Spirit. It turns out that as we surrender into self-denial, the emptiness changes into fullness, but a fullness of a different order than we are used to. Instead of a distracted fullness that ultimately leads to disorder and shallowness, the emptiness of spiritual self-denial grounds us and makes us whole. It gives us peace.

Self-denial should only be undertaken, however, with careful discernment. It helps to discuss it beforehand with a spiritual director or other wise soul, so that one does not take it on with steely resolve and self-punishment. For fasting of any kind is not some kind of bitter, hard work we must do in order to force ourselves into order, to finally get our lives "together." It is the gift of openness and vulnerability. It is a willingness to be weak and empty for a time, so that God can be for us a new kind of strength and fullness. It is a desire to be available for the work of God's loving grace.

Self-denial is profoundly contemplative, for it works by the process of human subtraction and divine addition. We subtract what is getting in the way, waiting in silence and emptiness. God adds grace and love in ways that we cannot obtain on our own.

Private Confession

Most of us who were not raised as Roman Catholics are only exposed to private confession through second-hand information, or what we see in the movies. Perhaps we imagine that confession is reserved for those who are dominated by shame and feel as if they must regularly expose the darkness of their hearts to a stern father figure. Or, we think that confession is only for the "really big" sins like adultery, embezzlement, or murder. Maybe we bristle at the idea that any human intermediary dares to stand between our conscience and God's forgiveness. Or, we have come to believe that therapy is the only appropriate relationship where we should expose ourselves in complete honesty about our secret faults and weaknesses.

Whatever the reason, if we never consider the healing power of this sacrament, now called the Rite of Reconciliation, we are missing a great deal. In reconciliation, we say out loud to another person those things that trouble us, whether they are specific things we have done at some time or more habitual in nature. As we lay it out on the table, what is normally in the dark is brought into the light and exposed to the grace of God. To do so in the presence of another person, normally a priest, makes us vulnerable and open, and it makes what we are saying that much more real.

Reconciliation is different from therapy in that the priest and the penitent do not normally engage in the kind of discussion that slowly uncovers historical background, motivations, parental influences, and other forms of insight. Instead, the penitent simply takes sincere and repentant responsibility for themselves by stating what they have done and what they have left undone, the priest offers brief counsel, and pronounces God's absolution.

So confession does not replace therapy, for therapy gets more at the kind of understanding that enables us to accept how we came to be the way we are. But neither does therapy replace confession, for confession moves beyond insight to action. We take responsibility for the ways our own wills and choices have led us astray, and for the ways in which we have perpetuated unhealthy patterns that originated long ago. We lay it out on the table in all humility, ask for God's forgiveness, and move on with our lives.

The rite does not act like magic; we do not rise up from absolution never to be tempted again by the things that bedevil us. Instead, in reconciliation we take a stance towards these things. We are able to say from this day forward "I have done my best to own up to who I am and who I am not, and I have received God's forgiveness for my failings." This perspective can be tremendously liberating, especially at particular times of transition in our lives, because it gives us a new way of handling our patterns of destructive and limiting thought and behavior when they do come up again in the future. As such, their power over us is diminished. We know that we do not have to be imprisoned by shame or habit, that God wants us to move into new life.

For contemplatives, the sacrament of reconciliation is helpful for all these reasons, but also for another one. In reconciliation, contemplative experience in a physical, direct, and acute way what they also do in silent prayer.

In prayer, we practice self-awareness. We watch our minds and learn about our habits of thought and emotion that keep us separated from God. We hold all this before God. So also in confession, we bring our habits, actions, and inaction out into the open, we say what they are to another person, and we formally receive God's love. We bring our self-awareness into the physical realm of relationship, the spoken word, and the touch of the priest's hand. Like all sacraments, reconciliation is a visible sign of an inward grace. We can do without the sign, just as we might know our union with Christ without ever receiving communion— but it can certainly help to use it from time to time.

Studying the Faith

Recently our parish went through a search process for a new director for our Contemplative Center, which offers groups, retreats, conferences, and other opportunities for contemplative formation as a sub-community of the parish and beyond. What we discovered in this process was a bit shocking. There are plenty of people who have been formally trained through various institutes of learning in the disciplines of spirituality, and are authorized to go forward as spiritual directors and leaders. But most of them have had little education in the fields of study that undergird and inform these spiritual disciplines: scripture, theology, church history, liturgy, church community life and service, and ethics.

One could say the same thing of many contemplatives who undertake a journey of spiritual growth within the life of the church. Seeking out only those offerings that have to do with prayer and the inner life of the Spirit, they may become skilled in particular spiritual disciplines, but they lack the undergirding of the church's teaching. It must be remembered that all the honored mystics and contemplatives in our history took for granted an ongoing education in the basics. They understood that their prayer lives could only be healthy and true if they were grounded in context. "Spirituality," as an isolated and self-contained way of being Christian, is a recent contrivance.

And so in order to be well-grounded, it is important for the contemplative to seek out, over the years, an education in scripture, theology, and all the rest. Most parishes offer plenty of opportunities for this education, but others exist outside the parish as well: diocesan schools, seminary programs for the laity, institutes, on-line courses, and, of course, books.[5] If classes are not available, most clergy are only too happy to work with a seeker who wishes to undertake a course of independent study.

When we study the Bible, we move away from a devotional and subjective way of approaching the text, where we ask the question "what does this passage have to do with my life right now?" to the more objective question "what is this text actually saying?" We discover its origins, audience, and historical context, its message and differences from other books of the Bible. We discover, for instance, that some of the Hebrew prophets who called down God's righteous anger upon the sinners might not have been taking aim at our everyday personal sins, but rather at their leaders' systemic, institutionalized oppression of the poor through exploitation, indifference, and cruelty. As such, these books of the Bible might help bring more clarity to our social, economic, and political life than to our individual moral life.

When we study theology, we discover that the issues debated over the centuries are not abstract philosophical concerns: they are about our lives. To say that Christ is both divine and human, each nature distinct and complete in itself, for instance, makes a difference. It tells us that God's presence in us never subsumes our imperfect humanity, and that our sin does not dilute God's presence in us, either.

---

5 An excellent resource in this regard is the New Church Teaching Series, published by Cowley Publications, which offers sound, approachable, contemporary books on the basic subjects of Christian faith and practice.

When we study church history and the lives of the saints, we find that whatever we may be struggling with in our own day has its precedents in the past. We might learn from their experiences. As an example, a study of the Reformation might give us some insights about our own attempts to balance the personal authority we bear for our own spiritual life together with the authority and wisdom of the corporate church.

When we study ethics and the application of our faith to our work and social life, we learn to challenge common assumptions about "the way things work," and apply different standards to how we must learn to treat one another.

For the contemplative, study of these subjects is critical, because in the practice of contemplative prayer, we are in relationship not just to a God of our own experience. We are in relationship to a God who has been known, described, and revealed to many who have come before. They have much to teach us about this God we pray to.

Further, we are in relationship to a God who calls us through prayer into engagement with a world that has a history, social problems, debates about how we should use our resources, and conflict over what life is really about. Contemplative prayer helps center us in the sure knowledge of God's presence, goodness, and love. The contemplative moves beyond that sure experience, through study and learning, into a clearer and fuller understanding of the Christian faith and tradition, in order to apply its wisdom to a faithful engagement with the world.

For the contemplative who seeks to grow through the traditional disciplines, study of the contemplative classics is especially important.[6] Many Christians do not

---

6 For a list of suggested reading in patristic and Eastern Orthodox sources quoted extensively in this book, see the Appendix.

even know that their own historical tradition includes a broad stream of contemplative saints and authors. Others know that lots of people are writing about spirituality today, but are ignorant of the history, thinking that we have only recently "discovered" an experiential, contemplative approach to faith.

A few years ago I attended a conference on medicine and healing, which ended up consisting of a number of doctors speaking to an audience of some nine hundred nurses, for the most part. They spent two days talking about "recent scientific discoveries" that show that healing can come through mind/body meditation, an experiential relationship with a higher power, and the unitive experience of an intercessor's compassionate spiritual presence with the sick. The bizarre thing is that they were talking breathlessly as if they and their colleagues had only recently discovered these things. There were no speakers offering wisdom from religious traditions that have been working with this for thousands of years.

This kind of fixation on the present day is endemic to our time. I have nothing against an emphasis on contemporary authors on prayer. In fact, the contemporary voice is often more accessible to readers than language that comes from a different time and place. Many historic authors, including some of the authors of scripture, present difficulties for the modern reader because they operated out of different assumptions about life, even different values. Sometimes the traditional sources seem musty, dense, and too romantic, scholastic, extreme, or authoritarian. The language of our day seems fresher and more immediate.

But our own contemporary way of speaking about faith is just as influenced by cultural assumptions and values. Right now we place a great deal of emphasis upon psychological insight, emotional support and affirmation, community, social justice, prosperity, and positive thinking, healthy human relationships, personal fulfillment, cultural diversity, and so on. Current spirituality reflects these values. What are often neglected in the spirituality of our day are such values as the transcendent power and mystery of the divine, a holy fear of God, confession of sin, self-forgetfulness, humility, sacrifice, and obedience to the church's traditional disciplines. In every period of history, religious writers wear cultural blinders. I wear them and am limited by them.

Contemplatives have been writing about their diverse experiences with the divine since the advent of religious literature. Within a linguistic style that is often foreign to our ears, there is great wisdom to be gleaned from these earlier authors. Early Christian contemplatives and theologians such as Origen, Gregory of Nyssa, John Cassian, and John Chrysostom speak eloquently of life in the Spirit. The desert fathers and mothers provide Zen-like, Jesus-like parables that surprise and awaken us. Monastic fathers such as Benedict, Basil, and Bernard of Clairvaux share with us their wisdom about community and the living of a balanced life.

Eastern writers from the fourth to the eighteenth centuries, principally found in *The Philokalia,* provide a consistently focused clarity about the practice of contemplative prayer. Nineteenth-century Russian masters including Bishop Theophan the Recluse patiently and lovingly offer to us, as they did to those simple people who came to them for guidance, a practical approach to the depths of devotional silence. Western medieval women mystics such as Teresa of Avila, Julian of Norwich, Catherine of Siena, and Hildegard of Bingen speak movingly about surrender and being radically open to the love of God. John of the Cross and the other Spanish mystics, Meister Eckhart and other German men and women mystics of the thirteenth and fourteenth-century Rhineland, Richard Rolle and his fellow Englishmen and women: all speak from the depths of hard-won spiritual wisdom.

More recent contemplatives include Therese of Lisieux, the Quakers, the Benedictine Dom John Chapman, Evelyn Underhill, Pierre Teilhard de Chardin, Thomas Merton, Anthony de Mello, and Bede Griffiths. Some excellent contemporary authors are Thomas Keating, Basil Pennington, Kathleen Norris, Monica Furlong, William Johnston, and the Orthodox bishops Kallistos Ware and Anthony Bloom.

The contemplative can benefit not only from reading authors from the Christian spiritual tradition. Taoist, Hindu, Sufi, Jewish, and Buddhist writings all can augment and shed new light on concepts that sometimes grow dusty and over-familiar for us when viewed exclusively through a Christian perspective. I am most familiar with the Buddhist tradition, and have benefitted greatly from reading Shunryu Suzuki, the Dalai Lama, Joko Beck, Pema Chodron, Thich Nhat Hanh, Jon Kabat-Zinn, Jack Kornfield, and others.

Christians sometimes wonder about the value of exposure to other faith traditions. I believe that it is important in the journey of faith to eventually come to a place of commitment to a particular tradition. We will forever stay on the surface until we stay put and dig deep within one discipline and its teachings, metaphors, and methods. In my own home state, Santa Fe is a notorious breeding ground for spiritual dilettantes, as well as the home for many deep and committed seekers.

But I also believe it is crucial for a person of any faith tradition to become informed about others, and to expose themselves to different ways of expressing the same reality that one's own faith tradition deals with.

I liken this to the fact that most of us live in a home, surrounded by particular mementos, furnishings, and living things that help us feel grounded in our lives, and even reflect back to us something of who we are. And yet we travel, we invite different people into our homes, and in other ways we bring the outside world into our homes so that we will be enriched. Similarly, we can live fully within our faith tradition, and also seek the enrichment and enlightenment of other traditions in a supplemental way.

Summary

The traditional disciplines of the Christian tradition offer much reward for the contemplative who learns to practice with them. In addition to silent meditation, one's personal prayer is augmented by the church's prayer in the form of the Daily Office. A greater sense of connection with others comes through intercession. The disciplines of fasting and almsgiving empty us in new ways and make us available to the loving grace of God. The sacrament of reconciliation makes physical and real our self-awareness. And in studying the faith tradition, our sights are lifted way beyond our own experiences to the wisdom of the holy ones who have gone this way before us.

Six

❁

Finding Support

FOR THE CONTEMPLATIVE IN THE CHURCH, life can be lonely. As enthusiastically as I have written about the spiritual opportunities and challenges of parish life in a previous chapter—remember I am a parish priest— I also know and understand the struggle of trying to maintain and develop a contemplative perspective and practice in a church environment that often does not understand or support it.

At clergy conferences and large church gatherings, I have learned to my surprise that many clergy do not really pray very much, that some consider the mystics to be strange, and that contemplative silence is seen as dangerous (because when we do not fill our prayer time with words, anything can happen!). I see parishes that are centered around activity, organization, service to people in need, or being a close "family." It is not that there is anything wrong with these things; they just do not provide, by themselves, much of an inspiration for the contemplative to be transformed in Christ.

I know that it is entirely possible to become superior-minded about this feeling of isolation: to think that only I see things from the unitive, mystical dimension, while all these other worldly, unspiritual slobs around me concern themselves with lesser things. But as long as we recognize this sinful and warped tendency when it arises, we can put it aside for the moment and return to the question of how the contemplative in the church may find support for what is often a lonely perspective.

Every parish offers worship, exposure to scripture, and opportunities for service. All church communities have people who inspire and challenge us to grow spiritually. Every local church communicates theology. Many congregations are good enough in terms of the basics. But not every place, in fact few, are equipped to provide, or are even interested in providing, the kinds of things beyond the basics that a contemplative also needs. This is not a reason to turn one's nose up at every parish until we find the "really spiritual" one that may exist only in our imaginations. It is simply a realistic understanding that we must work with a good-enough parish to provide us with some of what we need for our spiritual lives, not expecting it to be everything for us, and look elsewhere for the kind of support that our church community cannot or does not provide.

To seriously undertake and maintain a contemplative life, and to be guided through the pitfalls and difficulties that this life presents, we need help. We cannot do it alone. I have never known one healthy contemplative who does not have some kind of ongoing support along this challenging path. We need assistance from more experienced contemplatives in order to broaden our perspectives, suggest new approaches and resources, point out our errors, raise questions we had not considered, and to simply express different ways of seeing things. When we get mired or lost, we need compassionate understanding that can only come from real experience with the same. We need companions on the journey.

And so in this chapter I will suggest from my experience some resources that go beyond what the good-enough parish can usually offer: spiritual direction, a contemplative group, retreats and monastic communities, and reading. These kinds of resources are critical to the contemplative, not only in terms of providing personal support, but as a necessary part of the overall traditional context of what it means to be a Christian contemplative.

A Contemplative Group

Anyone who has spent time praying both at home alone and with a contemplative group knows that there is something qualitatively different about the two experiences. At home, we are private, and our way of being with God on any given day is determined within that privacy. Sometimes we are sleepy and have to rouse ourselves with chant, bowing, reading from scripture or praying aloud. Sometimes we must weep or sigh. Other times we raise our hands up in supplication, kiss an icon or light a stick of incense. Privacy in prayer is important, for ultimately we must encounter God on our own, in our own way, without any inhibitions.

In a group, by contrast, normally we sit very still and in complete silence, so that there is no one person who draws attention to themselves. In the stillness, the group of individuals may have their own private experience with God, but they also sit as a group, together. When a group of people remain completely still and silent, it is no longer just a collection of individual people praying; it is one corporate prayer. This togetherness is often palpable. It is the felt knowledge that we are in God, in this moment, all as one. Our minds may go in and out of awareness of this unity, we may for most of the time be more centered in our own individual prayer, but somewhere in the background is an awareness that we are here with God, now.

There is a power in this shared presence. Sitting with a few other people in complete stillness and silence can be awakening, arresting: it is as if we are suspended in the present with a heightened sense. There is also tremendous support in shared prayer. Sometimes people who are beginning to pray or who are going through a difficult time of crisis are not able to pray alone, and can only do so with the support of a group. Nothing needs to be said in this sharing; it is enough to sit together with hearts open to God. There is also accountability in a prayer group. We know that the group depends upon all of us being there, and we also know that our corporate prayer depends upon us sitting there faithfully through the time we have together.

A contemplative prayer group also has the opportunity to share experience. Sometimes the regular sitting time begins or ends with discussion, when participants share about their prayer and faith lives. Other times individuals in a group seek each other out before or afterwards, having conversation about their experience. In a group, there is often time for listening to a leader, or to audio or video tapes, who is more experienced on the contemplative path. This makes it possible to gain advice and insight in a way that cannot be found on one's own.

How does one find such a group? In many communities, Christian contemplative prayer groups just do not exist. In this case, it might be useful to join a meditation group of another tradition (Buddhist or Hindu, usually) if one exists nearby. You can orient your meditation towards God in prayer while others meditate in other ways. Many places have centering prayer groups now, which can be quite good. Centering prayer is one form of contemplation, and while it sticks to a fairly limited method and range of exposure to the broad Christian contemplative tradition, it is a good approach.

It is also possible to start one's own contemplative prayer group. It does not take a trained spiritual director or experienced teacher to lead one, as long as a few important guidelines are observed. A group can get together and follow a simple format: they can begin their time with one of the prayer book offices, sit in silence for a half hour or so, get up and walk together in a slow meditative walk in order to stretch the legs, sit again for another twenty or thirty minutes, and then end with another office or prayers from the Prayer Book.

When it gets together for prayer, the group can use *lectio divina* as a beginning point. This does not take a biblical scholar to lead it, but it does take a careful facilitator. In lectio, a passage from the scriptures is read slowly, silence is observed, and sometimes the passage is read a second time, followed by another silence. Discussion follows, which usually is most useful if individuals wait to speak until something from the scripture speaks to them, avoid personal intellectual opinions, and refrain from answering someone else's comment with their own. Another silence is observed before the next person speaks, so that all the comments come out of and return back again into a prayerful silence. The talking thus follows the rule of no "cross-talk" practiced both by Quakers and twelve-step recovery groups. Any capable clergy person can either provide facilitation guidelines or recommend someone in the community who can do so (perhaps someone with years of experience in twelve-step groups).

In addition, video or audio tapes can be used as a springboard for discussion. Sometimes our groups use short readings from the contemplative tradition, such as sayings of the Desert Fathers. But whether the resource is scripture or something else, the facilitator must be careful to guide the group according to agreed-upon ground rules. The facilitator should also have some ability to stop discussion when it goes astray from the purpose, and to recognize when someone is getting into an area that is better served by a therapist, a spiritual director or a clergy person, and to gently make such a recommendation.

A contemplative group should never become a support or therapy group. While its effect may be supportive and therapeutic, its method and goal is not. The technique and purpose is like that of spiritual direction: individuals share their experience of faith and prayer in an atmosphere where the Spirit, not the group, is recognized as the real guide for each. This makes it possible for strong feelings, deep insights, or confused perspectives to be shared openly without any need to direct, fix, or solve anything. What is said is heard, and then let go of so that God can receive and deal with what is offered.

I recommend that such a group remain firmly rooted in a parish, be approved of by the clergy, meet on the church grounds, and advertised regularly in the community. A contemplative group should never become privatized like a club, should always be easily accessible to anyone who wants to come, assuming they do not become disruptive, and be accountable to the clergy and people of the parish. Beginners should be regularly offered some orientation to the practice of the group. The advantage to meeting at the church is that it connects the group and their prayer in a concrete way with the wider community, its liturgy, intercessory prayers, and overall life and ministry.

In my parish, many years ago we started such a group, and it has grown over the years into what is now the Contemplative Center (CC)[1], offering a full range of support and opportunity for contemplatives. I offer a few comments about it here simply to suggest the kind of thing that is entirely possible in a parish, given the presence of a few people who care about developing such a ministry.

The CC is intended to be a sub-community of the parish, which is also open to the public at large. The participants in its programs come from parish membership and also from other churches in town; some others attend who are not otherwise a part of any faith tradition. The purpose of the CC is not just to offer a

---

1 For detailed current information on the CC, see our website at www.all-angels.com.

smattering of interesting spiritual classes and workshops, but to systematically build a community of contemplative practice within the context of parish life, which is rooted in our faith tradition.

At the center are a group of trained guides, who are committed to a common rule of life and who take part in an ongoing formation process with me and our director, reading and discussing from the Christian contemplative tradition. Guides not only facilitate group discussions, they also serve, as needed, as spiritual companions to participants in our programs, and assist the director and me in guiding the overall mission of the CC. The next widest circle are the oblates, who have committed to our common rule after six-months experience with it, and who also give input to the direction of our programs. Associates are those who are exploring our rule of life for a minimum of six months. "Companions" is the term we use for those who are a part of our community simply by taking part in some of our offerings from time to time, even if only once.

The rule of life we share includes a commitment to attending one of our two contemplative groups, one on an evening, one in the daytime; some of our quarterly Saturday half-day retreats; one of our two annual weekend retreats; and some of our quarterly public conferences, which feature outside speakers. It also includes a daily practice of contemplative prayer and one of the Daily Offices; weekly eucharist, a commitment to study in the contemplative tradition; work with a spiritual director; some form of self-denial; a willingness to live responsibly in community with church, neighborhood, and the natural world; a financial pledge to the parish or to the CC; and some kind of service to those in need.

I share this information not to impress or to advertise what we do, but to encourage and perhaps inspire those who wonder whether it is possible to build a contemplative practice in a parish setting with others. It is. It takes time, patience, the guidance of people who are experienced and well-educated in the overall faith tradition, and not just in "spirituality," and a gradual process of perseverance, discernment, and growth.

A group such as this can develop a new model of what it means to be a Christian in the world. Most of us are aware of the monastic model, where people live in community and practice prayer together. The problem with a non-monastic person seeking inspiration from this model is that they live a different lifestyle, one which offers every bit as much opportunity for prayer and growth in faith, but different nonetheless. Unless we become monks or nuns, we cannot fully share in that lifestyle. Most of us are familiar with the parish model, where people are united through corporate liturgical worship and ministry. The problem here is that those who are committed to a life of prayer do not get a whole lot of support from the usual parish activities.

But what is more rare is a community of people who regularly practice and learn about prayer together, who do not live together, but who are linked by obedience to a common rule of life based upon the traditional disciplines of the church, and who are nurtured and challenged by their participation in ongoing parish life. A simple parish contemplative group that only meets weekly, without all the offerings we have developed over the years, can provide such a community. This kind of community is not new to the church, there have been many kinds of third orders and lay communities of prayer. But I believe that right now, the time is ripe for its further development, especially for contemplatives.

Spiritual Direction

For many years, clergy were seen as the only "ministers" in a congregation, and the spiritual counsel they provided was often limited to pastoral care and comfort in times of crisis. Sometime in the latter half of the twentieth century, the American church began adopting all sorts of new roles for the clergy, casting about for their "real" identity: as social activists, administrative professionals, group facilitators, and religious therapists.

As the field of spirituality has mushroomed over the last few decades, many clergy and lay leaders have returned to the traditional role of spiritual director. While some of this return is no doubt due to the inevitable influence of faddish trends in the church, much of it is a genuine clarification of the unique role that a religious leader, ordained or lay, has. What else could be more important than accompanying or guiding the people of God in their spiritual journeys so that they may become more faithful Christians? What else was Jesus doing with his own disciples?

Among other duties, the leader, as spiritual director, simply works individually or in groups with those who are motivated to grow in faith. In doing so, he or she employs the traditional resources of prayer methods, scripture, confession, study, self-examination, and the discipline of a rule of life. Through these resources and others, the spiritual director inquires, probes, encourages, and provides insight for what is often a complex and difficult journey.

The director functions as witness to the directee's faith life. The real director is the Holy Spirit, and so the two people in this relationship exist in a triangle, with the Spirit providing the guidance that is needed. The director as witness raises questions, shares his or her own experience, and invites the directee to trust and move more deeply into the mystery of God, so that the Spirit might further guide and enlighten. The director need not, and should not, provide all the answers. The director's role instead is to humbly shepherd the directee God-ward, so that grace can do its work in the individual.

As such, the person who is receiving direction is ultimately responsible for his or her own growth in grace, for seeking and responding to the Spirit, and is not dependent upon the director.

In this sense the term "spiritual director" may not be the best one, because it suggests a hierarchy, where the expert is directing the novice towards some pre-conceived goal of spiritual accomplishment. Perhaps "spiritual guide" or "companion" would be more helpful. But I use the term "spiritual director" because it is widely understood, and because the tradition itself uses it. It is also true, even given what I have said about being simply a witness to the Spirit's grace, that the director should ideally be someone more experienced in prayer and wiser in faith than the directee. Mutual relationships of sharing are fine and often quite helpful, but they are not enough for someone who undertakes a practice of contemplative prayer. We need someone who has already been on the path we are walking on, and knows something about it.

Those who live in populous areas can usually find a spiritual director who is experienced in contemplative prayer, if they ask for God to help them, and they perservere in seeking. But many areas do not have such a person. What does the contemplative do then?

A creative approach to the problem includes many possibilities. Attending retreats in another geographical area or seeking out a referral, we may find someone out of town who is willing to be in touch by telephone or e-mail. A local spiritual director or pastor who is not a contemplative may nevertheless be wise enough in the faith to guide a contemplative directee. An open-minded teacher of meditation from some other religious tradition can be of great benefit. A peer relationship of sharing with another contemplative can help a great deal, as long as one also reads, attends occasional retreats, and seeks out other expertise.

A contemplative spiritual director of some kind can help a contemplative enormously. For it is here that one sees modeled the possibility of transformation in Christ. In this relationship, God's grace can become incarnated; it can take on flesh in the form of another caring, inquiring, concerned person. The contemplative journey can be difficult at times, and there is the real possibility that we can become discouraged or even lost along the way. We need not make it more difficult than it already is, and one way of making it easier is to humbly seek the guidance of another pilgrim who has been on this journey before us.

Retreats and Monastic Communities

Every contemplative should make some kind of retreat on a regular basis. This can be done in many ways. One can travel to monasteries either in local regions or different states and undertake a non-guided time of silence and participation in the community's daily round of worship. Some monasteries offer spiritual direction during retreatants' stays, others do not. Retreat centers, Buddhist centers and parishes, and some monasteries, provide structured retreat programs for groups, which can be especially helpful for those who have not yet taken a retreat. I have even known those who stay at home, unplug the telephone, television, computer, and radio, put away the car keys, and structure their day around daily offices, silence, reading, and meals.

Wherever one takes a retreat, one should consider certain factors that go into making what is uniquely a contemplative retreat. The term retreat is being used much more broadly than it used to be. Businesses, school boards, church groups, and corporations say they are having a "retreat" when they take a weekend or even just a day to plan their work. Spiritual groups commonly have the kind of retreat where they engage in teaching, discussion, writing, sharing, games, and other activities. Their time together is often busy, structured, and talkative.

There can be much good in this kind of retreat, but I would hesitate to call it contemplative. A contemplative retreat is more like what Anglo-Catholic and Roman parishes used to regularly offer when they called it a "silent retreat." A retreat master would appear wearing a cassock in the chapel after each of the daily offices and Eucharist, and offer one of a series of talks on a theme called meditations. Retreatants would then go off to their room, stay in the chapel and pray, or take a walk outside. Meals were in silence or someone read aloud from one of the spiritual classics. Spiritual direction and confession were provided as needed, but otherwise there was no conversation (or even eye contact) with anyone else. The only reading allowed was either assigned by the leader or from the Bible. One's time was spent chiefly in silent prayer.

A silent retreat such as this is a powerful source of support for the contemplative. Either alone or with others, a few days or a week of silence has an amazingly clarifying and strengthening effect. There is a cumulative momentum that builds over the days, moving one in a transition from busyness and distraction upon arrival, into what is often a period of struggle, questioning or seeking, and eventually into a place of peace, where one is rooted in the moment with an open heart and a clear mind. It does not always happen this way, but it often does.

Sometimes it is difficult to transition into the silence. We are generally so active in our lives that the lack of structure and noise can really throw us for a loop. We might spend the first day or two wandering around physically and mentally, unsure of what to do, or how to be. We might feel afraid of the silence. We might be sleepy, which can be a form of resistance, or it can also be a much needed call to rest. This period of disorientation is usually good, and often one of the ways that the Spirit works in us. Before we can be found we must be lost. Before the promised land we must wander in the desert. If this happens, just let yourself be lost, refusing to pick up books or other activity that will impose structure and take away what might be a important work of the Spirit.

This is where the availability of a spiritual director, monk, or some other wise presence can be helpful, even crucial, on retreat. Seek someone like this out if you need it, and if they are available. Try to stretch yourself by enduring the difficulty, but if things get too emotionally difficult, it might be more helpful to go home instead of forcing yourself to suffer through it. Sometimes it is not the right time to be on retreat.

When undertaking a silent retreat, it is essential not to carry much baggage along. Baggage can come in the form of lots of clothes, books, snack food, even religious paraphernalia. Instead, consider your retreat as an emptying journey into the desert, and follow Jesus' advice to his disciples to "carry no purse, no bag, no sandals" (Luke 10:4). Baggage can also come in the form of ideas about what is supposed to happen during the retreat, or a plan for what you are going to work on spiritually. It is usually much more useful to go with no agenda and remain open to the possibility that God may surprise you.

A retreat, like prayer, is really God's work in us more than it is our work. Our job is to open ourselves, invite the Spirit's presence, and not force something into being, trusting that God is indeed at work even if nothing seems to be happening. In my early years of taking retreats, I would often manipulate my own experience emotionally and spiritually so that something "profound" seemed to take place. Upon my return home, I would unsuccessfully try to communicate what had "happened" to my wife, who patiently listened and took it all with a grain of salt.

I would then find after a few days back in the world that I could not even remember the "breakthrough" that seemed so complete during the retreat.

Now I just go on retreat and let it be whatever it is. My job is to make myself available in the extended silence, and it is the job of the Spirit to do in me whatever needs to be done. While profound, moving, transformative experiences can happen on retreat, often the work of the Spirit is more subtle and hidden.

A mountaintop experience can be good, as long as we have not created it ourselves. But like Peter, James, and John on the Mount of Transfiguration with Jesus, we must go down the hill to the valley below where we live. We must jump back into our families, jobs, and our busy schedules. Sometimes retreatants experience a deep sense of grief upon their return, wishing that life could always be for them like it was on retreat, now feeling alienated from life as they live it.

What is to be done? It may be that changes in one's life do need to take place with the help of a spouse, friends, clergy, or therapist. It also may be that one needs to change one's idea of what is "spiritual" and what is not. A silent and peaceful retreat is not the only form of holiness. Holiness also take the form of meaningful and busy work, relationships of love, the creation of beauty in the home, redemptive suffering and struggle, and play. The question is whether we are able to move gracefully from the sacredness of silence and solitude into the sacredness of everyday life.

The thing that makes this possible is an ongoing practice of prayer. If this is not in place, then when we go on retreat we will have hard transitions both on the way in and on the way out, for it will be just too different from the way we live our lives. But if we do have a daily practice of contemplative prayer, then we will be able to flow in and out of a silent retreat with no difficulty, because we carry with us in our daily lives something of the same silence and peace throughout the day, no matter what we are doing.

Many contemplatives take their silent retreats at monasteries, which can be found by asking around, looking for Episcopal ones in your parish's copy of the *Episcopal Church Annual*, or searching the internet. Developing a relationship with a particular monastery is often a helpful form of support to contemplatives. This is accomplished by repeat visits over the years.

A monastery is usually a beautiful place. The geographic setting is often inspiring, remote, quiet, and therefore conducive to the pursuit of God. The furnishings and architecture are often spare and evocative. Spending retreat time each year in a familiar place of prayer such as this can help provide a spiritual "cue," just as a home altar does, that leads one into the depths of prayer more quickly and easily. When one is not even there, it can stand in the memory to serve the same function.

Because they have spent years dedicating themselves to prayer, contemplative monks or nuns can offer a wisdom and perspective that can be difficult to find elsewhere. The monastery is therefore one of the few places that one can go in our society today and have a reasonable chance of finding someone who can not only teach about contemplative prayer and experience, but also witness to its transformative effect on one's life.

Roman Catholic and Orthodox monasteries, like Anglican ones, offer hospitality to guests. Many times they post notices that non-Roman or non-Orthodox visitors should not receive communion.[2] If this is the case, and one is Protestant or Anglican, one should

---

2 Some Roman monasteries invite all to receive who share the belief with them that in the eucharist Christ is truly present. Episcopal communities of faith invite all baptized Christians to communion.

consider whether being included in the reception of eucharist is important enough to make one look elsewhere for a retreat site. Alternatively, some feel that God directs them in their conscience to just receive communion anyway, and they keep their religious affiliation to themselves. Some Roman monasteries prefer it this way.

Assuming we find a monastery that is suitable, we must look at how we see ourselves in relationship to it. Do we assume that the monks are holier than we are, than anyone who lives "in the world?" Monks do dedicate themselves to longer periods of prayer than most of us outside the monastery, but they live "in the world" as much as we do. They struggle with relationships, sin, resentment, worry, religious doubt, financial burden, and the distractions of many responsibilities. The retreatant who only sees the monks gliding in and out of chapel, glowing in their marvelous robes, has no idea about their actual humanity.

Spend some time and get to know them. They are just like you in most respects, including in their relationship with God. While some would rather keep their illusions about monastic sanctity, it does not do any good. Doing so only perpetuates a kind of dualism that posits a sacred place vs. secular places, sacred time and activity vs. secular ones, holy people and unholy people. This dualism keeps us stuck in the belief that we will never be able to find God in our lives. But God is everywhere, in all of us, just as available to all. Sin is everywhere, in everyone, and all must struggle to live into our redemption.

In fact, there are ways in which the monastery presents its own dark side, its own obstacles to spiritual growth, which outside the monastery walls are not such an issue. In the fourth century, the desert mother Amma Syncletia knew this very well, speaking of her community in contrast to the "seculars," who lived in cities:

We are like those who sail on a calm sea, and seculars are like those on a rough sea. We always set our course by the sun of justice, but it can often happen that the secular is saved in tempest and darkness, for he keeps watch as he ought, while we go to the bottom through negligence, although we are on a calm sea, because we have let go of the guidance of justice.[3]

There are ways in which the "rough sea," the everyday challenges of marriage, family, jobs, and demanding lifestyles can push us to seek God with greater vigilance than in the peace of a monastery.

One of the ways that a special relationship with a particular monastery may be shaped is through what some communities offer in the way of a program for associates or oblates. Many monasteries welcome this kind of connection, and information about whether they do may be requested. Normally, an associate undertakes a rule of life that translates the monks' various disciplines into a version that is more appropriate to a busier lifestyle. Regular visits to the monastery are encouraged, spiritual direction is offered there, and sometimes groups of associates meet outside the monastery in regional groupings. But even without the formal existence of this kind of program, a helpful support for the contemplative may be an ongoing relationship with a contemplative monastic community, developed by repeat visits.

Summary

In order to keep growing throughout one's life, the contemplative, like anyone else, must find support. A group of fellow seekers gives us a community of support

---

3 *The Sayings of the Desert Fathers*, Ward, 235.

that tells us we are not alone in our need for silence with God. A wise teacher, companion, or spiritual director helps us know ourselves more deeply and work through our particular struggles. Retreats and monastic communities provide an intense atmosphere for accelerated growth and focused attention.

None of this comes automatically to us as we go through life in the church, and in some sense it is hidden from view; for even though Buddhist and other forms of spirituality are much in popular evidence today, the Christian contemplative tradition remains obscure and unknown to most. And so we must seek it out; we must take the initiative. As we do so, one discovery leads to another, one conversation takes us into more, and one author introduces us to others.

It is important to remember that amid all these forms of support, amid all our efforts to find them, it is the Spirit who guides, supports, and enlightens. It is not all up to us to go out there and build up the depth and breadth we need. God will provide the support we require for our contemplative practice and transformation, if we genuinely desire it and make some effort. If we seek, we will find; if we knock, the door will be opened; if we ask, we will receive. On this we can rely.

✣

Part Three: Transformation

For the Christian, the purpose of faith and prayer is the transformation of our lives, so that they resemble the quality of being that Jesus Christ shared with us. He called this quality the kingdom of God, and promised that we could come to know it, in some measure, in our lifetime.

As we give ourselves to God through a practice of regular contemplative prayer, and as we live out this life of prayer within the context and support of the church, transformation—by the grace of God—takes place. We were created by God with great potential, and fulfillment of this potential is possible in Christ. "Be perfect [that is, whole, complete] as your heavenly Father is perfect," Jesus said (Matthew 5:48). Just before he died, he declared to his disciples, "I have said these things to you so that my joy may be in you, and that your joy may be complete." (John 15:11). Contemplative prayer is one way of moving, by grace, into this fulfillment.

The journey of transformation only beings in earnest, however, when we move beyond the initial delight of discovery into difficult arenas that challenge us deeply. Our prayer must become dedicated and disciplined. We must allow ourselves to be a bit lost at times, abandon our expectations about what is supposed to happen, and learn to practice contemplative awareness in all of our daily life. We must also move with prayerful contemplation into the heart of our difficulties, into suffering itself. Finally, by the grace of God, we are brought through this transformative journey into a kind of freedom that is not dependent upon circumstances, a holy detachment that paradoxically engages us in life more fully.

Seven

❈

Going Deeper

A FTER A NUMBER OF YEARS in parish ministry, my family and I took a five-month sabbatical in Mexico. After a month of traveling in our truck, we settled in a house in the city of Oaxaca, deep in the southern part of the country. We found that the further we had entered Mexico, the more we had a sense that we had left our familiar and comfortable world behind. By the time we got to Oaxaca, we were far into an adventure that had no simple or quick route of return. By virtue of a great expanse of land between our home and where we now found ourselves, we were fully committed.

From time to time this brought a little fear: what if our journey into this strange land turned dangerous or we became sick? What had we done? In fact, we turned out to be fine and most of Mexico actually felt safer than the United States, but still, there was the feeling that somewhere we had crossed the point of no return. And we did, at times, find ourselves immersed in difficult situations not of our choosing and beyond our control.

The contemplative journey has some similarities. At first, we enjoy the peace and quiet. We find it to be comforting. As we establish a practice of contemplative prayer, we feel newly centered and clear. We imagine that from now on we will be on a path of ever more clarity and peace. But like my family's adventure into Mexico, we find that over time, the contemplative journey is not simple, smooth, predictable, and straight. It takes us out of the familiar and comfortable into completely new and sometimes difficult territory. And once we have really committed ourselves, there is no turning back.

This is because in contemplative prayer we make ourselves available to God for transformation. I believe that as we do so, assuming we are ready for it, the Spirit takes our offer seriously, and begins to work on us. The subsequent conversion of our hearts is not a small matter that simply has to do with giving us a sense of tranquility. Sometimes in order to make us truly free, we are bound and "taken where we do not wish to go," as Jesus said to Peter about his future discipleship (John 21:18).

In order for God to transform us into the people we are created to be—loving, free, true, and holy—we must be taken to places that we would not ordinarily choose to go. Our habits of mind, heart, and behavior must be challenged and remade. Contemplative prayer is a workshop where this transformation, by the grace of God, can take place. The work that takes place here is ours, but the shape it takes is the Spirit's doing. Our cooperation is essential, but the outcome is beyond our control, for if we were the ones who were managing it, we would be able to transform ourselves.

How can we cooperate with this transformative journey that God wishes to take us on? We must do more than establish an initial practice of contemplative prayer. We also need to do more than practice this prayer within the overall context of the life and discipline of the church. We have to go deeper. We must learn to exercise both dedication and flexibility in our contemplative practices; we must move deeply into a loving relationship with God, who will nevertheless always remain a mystery to us; we must drop our expectations of what is supposed to happen in our spiritual lives; and we must allow our practices to move into our daily lives until nothing is left out, and all of it is touched by grace.

Dedication and Flexibility

Long ago, when I began to try to develop a closer relationship with God, I would pray and read the Bible from time to time. When I felt the desire to do so, I would spend a little while in silence, moving in and out of words as the Spirit moved me. Once a year or so I would go for a few days on retreat, when my prayer would become more sustained and frequent. But overall, I would tend to pray fairly irregularly. If I began to pray and "nothing happened," I would close it up and move on to the next thing. Days, sometimes weeks would go by and I would either forget or not feel moved to pray. The result was that I was always beginning at the same place, sometimes lurching a little forward, but then drifting backwards again.

Imagine if someone who wanted to dance beautifully took this approach. Stretching now and then, practicing the traditional positions, leaping a little when they felt like it...but then dropping it when they didn't feel like practicing. We know what the result would be. They would never feel the exhilaration of moving beautifully, with strength, flexibility, and grace. They would always be hindered by their lack of discipline.

The early spiritual authors spoke of *askesis*, often translated as "practice," or more accurately, as "asceticism." We tend to think of this latter term as referring to those bizarre examples of stylites who perched on pillars for years on end, or the Celts who submerged themselves up to their necks in icy water during meditation. But the original sense of *askesis* was that of an athlete (this word also comes from the same Greek root) who was engaged in a discipline of progress.

Viewed this way, we can understand it more easily. While few of us are real athletes, many of us know what it is to sustain a discipline of physical conditioning. We may run, swim, or do aerobics regularly, or tone our muscles through the lifting of weights. We know that when we are inconsistent in our discipline, our bodies go back to their pre-conditioned states. When we are consistent, we feel the benefits of more flexible, trimmed, and stronger bodies, greater vitality, even a clearer mind.

We may say that we want the benefits of a spiritual life: greater love for others, gratitude for this moment in creation, open hearts and clear minds. But are we willing to undertake the ascetical discipline, the training that is necessary? Are we just as willing to put in the hours of spiritual practice as we are to go to the gym?

Perhaps it is easier to exercise physically because many others do it, or because we can feel the results more quickly. Perhaps it is harder to sustain a discipline of prayer because it takes us first on a path of obvious benefits (greater peace, relaxation, openness) but then leads us into some of the difficulties of transformation (confrontation with our demons, our limiting habits of mind and heart).

But if we do sustain a discipline of daily prayer, we will find, over time, that the benefits come. Transformation does work away at us, and we get to a point when we realize that we would not think of going a few days without prayer, any more than we normally would go a few days without eating. It becomes our sustenance, a necessary part of staying sane, happy, open, healthy, and free. Eventually, it also becomes the very means we rely upon to attain healing from life's struggles and pain; it is the way we move from death to life.

And so *askesis* is the spiritual training we must undergo in order to progress in the life of faith. Asceticism is the necessary discipline of silence, scriptural reflection, sacrament, study, and all the other traditional practices. Just as athletes or musicians must practice day in and day out, whether it is raining or snowing on their jogging route, whether they feel like it or not, we too must learn to take ourselves into prayer day in and day out, even when we do not feel like it. Like other disciplines, we pray without expecting immediate results, confident that our dedication will result in good things over a long period of time.

There is something liberating about not expecting every time of prayer to be a wonderful experience. Without this expectation, we can "just do it," knowing that the training will pay off in the long run, that we are in it for the long haul. This frees us because then we can just do the prayer and trust that something larger than our immediate experience is at work. We can have faith that God hears our prayer no matter what we are feeling, honors it, and moves us, over time, wherever we need to be. We need not worry about how well we're doing in the moment. We can just pray. In this regard Martin Thornton uses the analogy of cleaning a car:

> When we are lucky enough to have a new one we wash and polish away with enthusiastic fervor; it is a devotional job. When the novelty wears off it becomes rather a nuisance and rather a bore, but we can still clean it efficiently, and here is the one vital point; there is no difference whatever in the result. It is exactly the same with prayer.[1]

At first, prayer is exciting and rewarding. Then in dry times, we just do the work of prayer, without feeling much reward. There is nothing glamorous about an ongoing practice of contemplative prayer. Much of the time we are just sitting there. But as Thornton points out, when we "just sit there" with as much faith as we have, the result, thanks to the grace of God, is just the same as if we "felt" something devotionally. Discipline and dedication are the necessary ingredients of our part in the relationship with God; the results are up to the Spirit.

---

1 Martin Thornton, *Christian Proficiency*, (Cambridge: Cowley Publications), 4.

But there is also an inherent problem with dedication and discipline. Many of us are driven by perfectionism. We want to be good boys and girls; we want to fulfill our duty and not disappoint anyone, especially God. But we are not robots, and so there are times when we just cannot maintain a perfectly disciplined spiritual life. We then condemn ourselves for not getting up every single morning at the same time and being rigorous about our prayer.

Because none of us feels holy, loving, and free all the time, we carry around a background sense of failure, believing that if we were really disciplined, we would be experiencing all these fruits of prayer all the time. We then rededicate ourselves with greater vigor, determined not to fail. And so we swing back and forth between zeal and guilt. With perfectionism, prayer ceases to be a fluid, lively experience; it becomes a duty.

Keep in mind that prayer is, above all, a relationship with God. Like all relationships, our relationship with God can be untidy. Life is messy. We all know that in a marriage or friendship, it is deadly, and would be ridiculous if it were not so destructive, when people insist on perfection in their relationship: perfect communication, sex, attention, sensitivity, and fairness. We know that, as humans, we are not ever going to be that neat, and that our relationships are an evolving and inconsistent process.

While it is easy to understand this in terms of human relationships, we somehow cannot accept it about our relationship with God. We expect of ourselves perfect discipline, consistency, faithfulness, clarity, commitment, detachment, and devotion. Imagine if we expected that of anyone else in our lives! Why do we expect it of ourselves in relation to God? Perhaps because we are afraid, because we cannot really believe that God loves us fully as we are today, with no improvements, with no further "progress" spiritually. Of course, God wants us to grow and transform, but this desire is situated in the context of complete, unconditional love for us as we are this very moment.

What this means for a contemplative practice is that while we must be on guard against a sloppy or inconsistent practice, we need not be anxious about doing it all right. If we honestly and humbly open our hearts to God as frequently as we can, over time the Spirit will guide and transform us. The important thing is to be available to grace, for it is grace that saves us, not our own efforts. Being a perfectionist contemplative will accomplish nothing, if we are relying on our own intelligence, insight, discipline, will, and other natural and acquired abilities. It is grace that transforms us, within the relationship between us and God.

What is important is to remember that we are only human. Our contemplative lives will never be perfect, and we must muddle along, seeking a more devoted and effective way of praying, to be sure, but knowing in all our efforts that we can always rest in God's loving assurance that by grace, our devotion will be honored, and we will be given what we need in order to be brought more fully into the kingdom of heaven.

My wife's cousin undertook years of serious meditative practice as a young adult. He believed that he needed to take seriously the discipline of sitting completely still, no matter what. Having a large, relatively inflexible Western body, he did so to his own physical detriment. His legs now are permanently damaged, always feeling somewhat numb and tingly. While he grew up playing basketball, he can no longer do so.

But a macho approach to prayer is not just physical. There are those who try to sit through exhaustion or emotional distress in a way that only makes matters worse. There are those who have no business just sitting with great grief or anxiety. What they need instead is conversation, understanding, compassion, therapy, medication, or rest. Sometimes I wonder if some of the visions and other extraordinary experiences of the saints in ages past were the results of mental and emotional overload, borne out of long hours, days, and months of unbending spiritual discipline in the face of isolation, sleep deprivation, hunger, illness, desperation, and confusion.

While we may not put ourselves in a cloistered situation, we do, at times, burden ourselves with inhuman expectations regarding prayer. I do believe that it is important, especially for us generally lazy and coddled Americans, to push ourselves beyond our comfort levels and personal preferences. We must learn to get up and pray in the morning when we would rather stay in bed, to go to church and receive the sacrament when we would rather avoid the community, to fast from self-indulgence, and to look at things about ourselves that arise in the silence when we would rather avoid it by blissing out.

But having said this, it is also important to really listen to what our body and our feelings are telling us. If I have had several tiring days and a long evening meeting, I'm probably not going to get up at 5:30 in the morning just to sit through exhaustion and a mental fog. My relationship with God is better served if I sleep a little longer and wake up next to my wife, and then move gently into the day.

It is a question of balance between dedication and moderation. Over time we must pay close attention to, on the one hand, our resistance to discipline, and on the other hand, our physical and emotional needs and limitations. Somewhere in this discernment we will find the way forward, and remember that while we are truly called to struggle into transformation, we are also human.

In the fourth century, Anthony the Great was visited by someone who expressed shock that he was not more strict with his disciples. Anthony said "Put an arrow in your bow and shoot it." So he did. Anthony said "shoot another" and he did so. Then he said "shoot yet again," and the visitor said "if I bend my bow so much I will break it." Anthony said "it is the same with the work of God. If we stretch the brethren beyond measure they will soon break. Sometimes it is necessary to come down to meet their needs."[2]

Intimacy and Unknowing

Usually when we begin a serious practice of prayer, we do so not only because we feel called to it, but because we feel some rewards in doing so. We feel the presence of God in new ways as we pray; our lives become more filled with an intimate sense of the Spirit. We love God, and we know that God loves us. Prayer, then, is something joyful to which we want to return day after day. When we feel drawn to devote ourselves more fully to prayer and faith, it is as if God responds to this impulse by seducing us. God reaches into our prayer, our everyday consciousness, even our dreams, and gives us wonderful, satisfying gifts: peace of mind, clarity of thought, gratitude, freedom from our attachments. God tells us that we are loved, and we express our love for God.

We think this will last forever, but it doesn't. The sense of presence fades into a sense of absence. It is as if God wants to hook us into a relationship with a taste of what we might get from that relationship. And then God seems to withdraw, no longer playing the seducer. God seems absent, and the gifts we enjoyed are no longer there. Why is this? Is God playing games with us, teasing us with possibilities, and then denying them to us?

---

2 *The Sayings of the Desert Fathers*, Ward, 3.

St. John of the Cross is one of the clearest voices who speaks to this dilemma. His message is that God works in this way deliberately, in order to first draw us in through intimate experience, and then to free us from dependency on experience. God gives us a knowledge of the divine, and then moves us beyond our limited capacity to know, into unknowing.

John's term, the dark night of the soul, is regularly misunderstood in spiritual circles. It is usually taken to mean any form of difficulty or depression, when John of the Cross had a much more specific thing in mind. He was talking about the movement from a seemingly successful prayer life that inexplicably loses meaning and comfort. When this happens, we are plunged by the grace of God into unknowing, where every spiritual exercise from which we formerly derived great meaning now becomes dry and lifeless. John likens this process of grace to weaning:

> When God sees that they have grown a little, he
> weans them from the sweet breast so that they
> might be strengthened, lays aside their swaddling
> bands, and puts them down from His arms that
> they may grow accustomed to walking by
> themselves. This change is a surprise to them
> because everything seems to be functioning
> in reverse.[3]

This sense of failure, surprise, regress, and loss is, for John, a sure sign of a call to the depths of contemplative prayer. Rather than it being a sign of failure or regression, the end of initial intimacy with God is a sign of progress. We are being weaned from dependency upon experience and "knowing," into mystery and unknowing. It is a

---

3 *The Collected Works of St. John of the Cross* (The Dark Night Ch. 8), trans. Kieran Kavanaugh, O.C.D., and Otilio Rodriguez, O.C.D. (Washington DC: Institute of Carmelite Studies, 1973), 312.

normal, expected part of the journey of faith. Its purpose is to make us more dependent upon God in faith, and less dependent upon our knowledge and our experience.

Most of us are relatively pleasure-driven humans who will not pursue too much of anything unless it feels good. We also will not pursue something we do not understand. God knows this, and initially uses it to draw us in. We are given pleasant, seemingly understandable experiences. But God also knows that when we insist on pleasure and understanding, we end up in idolatry. In our relationship with God, when we depend upon rewards for our efforts, we are really more interested in the rewards than the relationship. This is idolatry; it replaces God with something less. As a spiritual director told me long ago "I think you may be more interested in your experiences of God than you are interested in God."

God is insistent that we not limit the divine to anything. God refuses to be named, defined, owned, or manipulated. God weans us from certain experiences, which are inevitably very limited in nature, so that we may remain radically open to whatever God might be in this moment. By refusing to be identified with this or that experience, God remains free and beyond our tiny capacities to comprehend. After all, if God could be understood or predictably experienced, then God would be as small as our understanding and our experience. But God is infinite, and beyond all comprehension.

When God weans us from dependency on initial spiritual experience, we learn to pray more humbly, making our offerings to God, not asking for anything for ourselves, not even asking to understand or perceive God in our prayer. St. John gave advice to those who find themselves in this position:

> They must be content simply with a loving and peaceful attentiveness to God, and live without the concern, without the effort, and without the desire to taste or feel him…for contemplation is

nothing else than a secret and peaceful and loving inflow of God.[4]

And so there is a movement in the contemplative life from intimacy to unknowing, from presence to absence, from fullness to emptiness. It is all part of the journey, and there is not one point along the path where we will remain forever. While I have described here a process that frequently (but not always) occurs early on in the contemplative journey, it is not limited to the beginning. For the contemplative life is one that is marked throughout by both a loving intimacy with God and also a patient waiting in emptiness.

This is not a contradiction; it is a paradox. We usually think of love as one thing, which feels pleasant and has a sense of mutual response, and emptiness as another thing, which feels unpleasant and desolate. But when it comes to God, we can love without knowing the object of our love, without receiving any signs of the presence of our beloved. We can just love, without demanding any reward or visible response. These two stances of love and emptiness can even be simultaneous, as we hold ourselves in loving devotion before the wondrous Source of all, before the One who is also shrouded in mystery and silence, beyond all knowing and perceiving.

The paradoxical experience of intimacy and unknowing are central to all the contemplative saints of the Christian *via negativa* (or *apophatic*, self-emptying path). God is beyond all our comprehension and never confined to our feelings in prayer, but also intimate, loving, and loveable. St. John of the Cross, again, is a good example of the *apophatic* tradition. His personal motto of faith was *Nada, Nada, Nada* ("Nothing, Nothing, Nothing"). But he also wrote passionate poems about his love for God:

---

4 *Ibid.* (Ch. 10), 317, 318.

How gently and lovingly
You wake in my heart,
Where in secret you dwell alone;
And by your sweet breathing,
Filled with good and glory,
How tenderly you swell my heart with love![5]

The contemplative life, then, involves both intimacy and emptiness. There are times when we pour out our hearts to God in devotion, times when we just sit in simple availability, times when God seems to respond to our love, and times when God seems far away. There are times when we can hold ourselves in loving devotion that is directed towards *no-thing*. This paradox of love and emptiness is at the core of the contemplative tradition. Christian contemplation is not a practice of cold, unfeeling detachment; it is a passionate love affair with the Spirit. But Christian contemplation is also not dependent upon emotional experience, either; it is a love whose mysterious object cannot be captured and held.

How do we nurture this paradox in prayer? How can we actively love God in prayer, without knowing or feeling the object of our love? Our tradition is full of helpful guides along the way. The psalms are a rich resource in this regard; they point to yearning as a way to be both loving and empty, intimate and unknowing. For it is the nature of spiritual yearning to feel our love for God, and yet also to know that the object of our love cannot be possessed. Hear the ancient voice of prayer in the wonderfully contemplative, *apophatic* psalms:

You speak in my heart and say "seek my face,"
your face, Lord, will I seek. (27:11, BCP)

---

5 Ibid. (The Living Flame of Love), 718.

As the deer longs for the water-brooks,
so longs my soul for you, O God.
My soul is athirst for God, athirst for the
living God;
when shall I come to appear before the
presence of God? (42:1–2, BCP)

For God alone my soul in silence waits,
from him comes my salvation.
For God alone my soul in silence waits,
truly, my hope is in him. (62: 1, 6, BCP)

O God, you are my God, eagerly I seek you;
my soul thirsts for you, my flesh faints for you,
as in a barren and dry land where there is no
water. (63:1, BCP)

My soul waits for the Lord,
more than watchmen for the morning,
more than watchmen for the morning. (130:5)

Our yearning for God is born out of an experience of absence. We tend to see this as something negative, as if there is something wrong with us if we cannot sustain a happy, positive, grateful, and full awareness of God all the time. But absence has its place, and the psalms call us into it. It is in the absence that we are most aware of the futility of all our spiritual fullness. It is there that we understand that our "spirituality" is often just a lot of pious noise. It is there that we come face to face with our helplessness, our fragility. It is in the absence that we must surrender and die, even to the ego constructions of spirituality.

When this happens, a deeper contemplation begins. For in the sheer silence of unknowing, yearning is awakened, our raw need for nothing except God. We know, in this place, that no thing, no "experience" will satisfy. Only God will do, and we are utterly dependent on grace. It is in the yearning itself that God becomes known, because God can only be seen and heard when everything else is out of the way. When we are naked and only our yearning, our raw faith remains, then God is no longer obscured. Gregory of Nazianzus described how our desire for God leads us into emptiness, and how this emptiness leads us back to intimacy with God:

> ....in so far as we fail to understand [God] he
> may excite our curiosity;
> this will awake in our soul the longing to
> know him further;
> this longing will lay bare our soul;
> this nakedness will make us like God.
> When we have reached this state, God will
> converse with us as friends.
> ~ *Oration* 45, for Easter

And so it is not as if the yearning in silence is only a means to the end, which is satisfaction in God. Yearning itself is an experience of the divine. Gregory of Nyssa speaks of the soul longing for God in his commentary on the Song of Songs, that beautiful and erotic poem of human love in the Hebrew scriptures, which has served as an allegory for the mystic relationship of love between God and the soul. In a passage that describes the seemingly unfruitful search of the bride for the bridegroom, the search of the soul for God, Gregory wisely points out that the search itself is the fulfillment:

> The veil of her grief is removed when she learns
> that the true satisfaction of her desire consists in
> constantly going on with her quest and never
> ceasing in her ascent, seeing that every fulfillment
> of her desire continually generates a further desire
> for the Transcendent.[6]

---

6 From *Glory to Glory*, Danielou and Musurillo, 270.

No Expectations

In our culture we are inundated with images and stories of the lure and promise of success. The ideal is held forth: set your goals, become who you want to be, apply yourself, make progress, achieve results. Be wealthy, thin, positive, beautiful, strong, productive, fun, effective, and a good lover. It is difficult to live in our culture and not be influenced by this message.

It used to be that men were the ones who were primarily subject to the lure of success, with our self-worth being based inordinately upon it. But now that women are a major part of the professional work world, they too are affected. We are all looking in the mirror, looking at each other, hoping we are moving forward like we should. When we fail, it strikes at our core; our self-worth comes into question, because we are not measuring up to our expectations.

In this environment it is easy to apply this same worldly view of ourselves to our faith lives. We measure "how we're doing," marking our progress in grace and freedom, even evaluating each session of prayer as good or bad. We carry an expectation that as we apply ourselves to prayer and worship, to study and service, that we will move forward in achieving the desired results: peace, joy, freedom, love. There is some truth to this view, and we should be confident that as we conform ourselves to God's life within us, grace will, over time, move us forward into the kind of life that Jesus promised: "I came that they may have life, and have it abundantly" (John 10:10). "I have said these things to you so that my joy may be in you, and that your joy may be complete" (John 15:11).

But our prayer lives should be, at the same time, free from anxiety about how we are doing. As we devote ourselves to a practice of contemplative prayer over time, it is important to do what we do, and leave the results to God. It is important to learn detachment from both success and failure, and stop looking at ourselves in the mirror. Our gaze should be fixed on God instead, so that eventually we care more about God than our expectations of what prayer and faith are supposed to "do for us."

This is an issue of faith, of trust. In constantly measuring ourselves and our sense of progress, we are really trusting in our own obedience, faithfulness, and effectiveness in prayer to get us where we expect to go. When we feel successful, we might believe that this is a result of our efforts, and when we feel a failure, we often believe that we have not done enough.

Faith in God has a different approach. It says that it is our job to be as faithful as we can, and it trusts God to transform us into the people we need to be. Faith asks us to step outside the whole arena of success and failure and to let go of all expectations, so that God can be free to do whatever work is necessary.

This is especially hard to do when our prayer does not seem to "work," when in spite of our faithfulness, we still find ourselves stressed out, lonely, anxious, or depressed. This is when it is hardest to trust in the grace of God, and to let go of our expectations. We beat our heads against the wall, saying "but I'm doing everything I'm supposed to, and it still isn't working." But it is in this very place, in our failure, frustration, and our difficulty, that we learn to trust, not in our successes.

This becomes an issue when after some months or years of practicing prayer, we move from initial intimacy with God, from initial "success," to a sense of absence and dryness. We are disappointed in ourselves. We seem to have returned to square one, having made no progress. We do not know how to move forward, and we feel like we are still just beginners. This feeling is a good thing, actually, because we are all beginners in prayer. After all, God is God, and we are only human.

There is no such thing as an "expert," who never feels lost or incompetent in prayer. And when we do feel like we know what we are doing, that is usually the time when God withdraws from us and lets us twist in the wind for awhile. As stated by Shunryu Suzuki in his book *Zen Mind, Beginner's Mind*, we must return, again and again, to that place where we know that we are always a beginner. We must know that we do not know. We must simply be humble, open and still, so that God can then be new for us again.

Our relationship with God in prayer depends upon humility. We must always remember that it is God who saves us and not we ourselves. In a wonderful story of Abba Moses, it was said that an important magistrate went to see the famous old man. When he found a monk from whom he could ask directions (it was Abba Moses himself, unbeknownst to the magistrate), the old man said "What do you want with him? He is a fool."[7] We are all fools when it comes to holiness.

We do not have to sustain "successful contemplative prayer," whatever that is; we just have to do what we can to be open, and humbly leave the rest to God. After some months or years of practice and we hit a time of aridity, this is the time to just keep on praying and leave the results to God.

Aridity is natural in the life of prayer. Aridity is natural in any relationship, and it does not mean that we have failed. There are just times when nothing spectacular or particularly comforting seems to be happening. And yet like in any relationship of love, the grace of mutual presence, going about one's business through life together, somehow results in a deepening of love. We must learn to trust that God is at work at all times, even when nothing seems to be occurring.

---

7 *Sayings of the Desert Fathers*, Ward, 140.

On a continuum that stretches from the worst sinner to the greatest saint, there may seem to be great differences, from our point of view. Some seem to be spiritual failures, others great successes. But the glory of God is way beyond this continuum altogether, and the kingdom of God of which Jesus spoke so much had a way of inverting it altogether. "Many who are first will be last, and the last will be first," he said (Matt. 19:30). It is better for us if we drop the whole notion about being good or bad at prayer, advanced or beginners in contemplation, and just pray.

But what about when things get really hard? When not only our expectations of constant progress go unmet, but when things fall apart? What is the role of contemplative prayer during dark times?

When we face real difficulty, we enter into the presence of what can potentially become our greatest teacher.[8] When we feel stuck, abandoned, confused; when we are sick or in pain, when terrible life circumstances absorb all our attention and energy; when we cannot think of anything other than what we are going through; this is when contemplative prayer seems most impossible, and yet when it also becomes most useful. What is required of us in these times is a radical willingness to let go of all our expectations and disappointments, and learn to be present to God in every circumstance, even this. What is necessary is that we learn to accept that our difficulty is prayer, too.

Contemplation teaches us how to sit still, how to be present to whatever is happening in our minds, our emotions, in our lives. Contemplation helps us accept and fully experience our lives as they are. When things are not at all what we expect or want them to be, either in our lives in general or in a particular time of silent

---

8 Suffering can so powerfully move us more deeply into the contemplative life of faith, that the next chapter is devoted to it entirely.

prayer, contemplation teaches us to just be with what is, without judgment, without any effort to change it. This is hard. But as we practice being present to what is, we gradually discover that this difficulty is not as powerful as we imagine. We find that God is still God, and life is still holy, and we are not destroyed. In fact, we discover that pain itself can be the gateway to a genuine freedom and joy that is not hindered by any of life's circumstances.

Contemplation does this by having us sit still, feel our difficulty, and hold it before God as an offering of where we are in this moment. As we do so, as we let go of our expectations of how life or prayer is supposed to be and just offer who we are in this moment, we find that our difficulty is not all that we are. We sense an infinite container in which our difficulty is held, a container that accepts what we feel and also says "there is more than your difficulty." When we discover this wider perspective, we find our freedom in God. We transcend the prison of the self and all its concerns, and move again into God's life. Our experience then becomes not so much about me and my difficulty, but about God.

As long as things are going well for us, as long as prayer meets our expectations, we remain dependent upon good fortune and spiritual success. But when things fall apart and our expectations are unmet, and when we hold this too as an offering before God, without judgment or expectation of change, we have a chance of discovering the God who is not limited by circumstance. We have the opportunity to discover a freedom that will not be controlled by good or bad, by darkness or light, even by life or death.

This is not to say that we should always just accept whatever is happening, and embrace whatever we are feeling. Sometimes we need to change things, to take action, to examine the rut or the danger we are in, and seek help. We must be discerning about this, often with the help of a spiritual director, a friend, or a therapist.

Depression is a common affliction in our day, and serves as a good example of how we must practice discernment between contemplative acceptance and direct action. There is a big difference between clinical depression and depressive feelings that are natural to all humans. The former needs professional attention; the latter is simply a part of life, and need not always be medicated, in spite of what the advertisements from the pharmaceutical companies tell us. All of us feel sad, somewhat hopeless, and blue at times.

Contemplative prayer is not the cause of either clinical depression or of depressive feelings. But it can exacerbate both. A person who is clinically depressed is not going to be helped by erroneously thinking of this condition as a "dark night of the soul." Silence, solitude, and remaining still in the point of despair are not the solutions, and it may make matters worse. People who simply feel blue from time to time do not feel that way because they sit in contemplative prayer. But they can sink further into the pit if they just sit through it passively, brooding on the cloud that envelops them. Perhaps what they need at these times instead of deadly-serious silent time of prayer is a friend, a meal out, a coffee and newspaper at a sidewalk café, a little music... a little action, a little life.

On the other hand, it can be useful to sit through our dark moods and occasional feelings of despair, if that is all they are. When we come to the end of our distractions, work, friendship, entertainment, we must simply go into the inexplicable sadness and just feel what we feel in God's presence. In fact, we will know if this is what we need if we are able to sink down into the mood and eventually find, underneath all our thoughts and emotions, a kind of deep peace at the root of it all. For in spite of our ups and downs, God still is.

The desert fathers worked through their own depressive moods with the tool of contemplation. They were affected by what they called the demon of accidie (or "the sickness that lays waste at mid-day," from Ps. 91). In the long hours of the hot desert silence, you can imagine a creeping sense of pointlessness, even of despair. But they brought this, too, to prayer, and discovered a peace that lay beneath their despair. Evagrius, one of the pioneers of the fourth-century desert monastic tradition in Egypt, concludes a discussion on accidie with this hopeful note:

> No other demon follows close upon the heels of this one (when he is defeated) but only a state of deep peace and inexpressible joy arise out of this struggle.[9]

Perhaps the peace and joy of which he speaks comes from the experience of having come to the experiential understanding that our difficulties are only a paper tiger: they have no ultimate power, and are simply passing phenomena. Underneath these passing experiences is our real life, our eternal groundedness in God. Sometimes we can only come to this reality by sitting through what we believe to be real, so that we can remember again that it is not.

Faith is a journey, and on this journey the scenery changes all the time. Peace gives way to conflict, clarity to boredom, despair to certainty, stillness to chaos and back again to stillness again. The Spirit is alive, moving through our lives in ways that are responsive to the moment. We are alive, responding and reacting to a whole range of stimuli in ways that we cannot control. Nothing stands still. Contemplative prayer is a real relationship, with ups and downs. It is a process of becoming, guided and upheld by the love of God. This, and perhaps this alone, is what can be the foundation of a realistic and hopeful expectation for the life of prayer.

---

9 *Sayings of the Desert Fathers*, Ward, 19.

Life as Prayer

I have spoken of some the things that help us in going deeper in contemplative transformation: being dedicated and also flexible; living in the paradox of an intimate relationship with the unknowable mystery of God; and moving through our expectations to a place of just being with God, as we are. For the most part, these things are all about our practice of prayer.

But if our contemplative life is limited to intentional periods of prayer alone, it will always be limited. To move even deeper, we must allow our contemplative practice to expand beyond the boundaries of intentional prayer, into every dimension of our lives, until every part is eventually touched and transformed. Nothing, in the end, is left out. Every moment of how we live will be affected by contemplation. For the point of a contemplative life is not to have wonderful experiences of prayer; it is to allow the transformation of our actual lives, so that we become, by the grace of God, more faithful, loving, just and free in all that we do. Our life itself must become a prayer so that the world may benefit from our transformation.

One way to allow prayer to permeate one's whole day is by interspersing it with intentional prayer. The Daily Offices help in this regard, because they interrupt the momentum of activity, and put us squarely in an awareness of God's presence, so that we are then more likely to remember just where we are in between the offices. This, of course, is the principle of Christian monastic, Jewish, and Islamic prayer that stops all activity at certain points during the day and turns to God in worship.

In a similar vein, there is also the practice of spontaneous prayer, which quaintly and problematically used to be called ejaculatory prayer, that shoots little phrases or sentences of worship or intercession out to God whenever the need arises: "Lord, have mercy," "O God, protect us as we drive," "Help me to bring harmony to this meeting," "Thank you for the blessing of this beautiful day."

These traditional practices are very effective ways of filling in the time between contemplation, worship, and other more extended periods of prayer, so that more of our lives are imbued with an awareness of God's presence. But what about the time in between these moments of intentional prayer? What about the kind of consciousness we have all day long? What about all those moments and hours when we are daydreaming, worrying, planning, doing, speaking, thinking, feeling, getting things done? Can this be prayer as well?

What these questions raise for the person of prayer is the hopeful possibility that our consciousness can be transformed so that as we go through any activity or circumstance in life, we are still able to bring contemplative awareness to it. Now what often comes to mind when this sort of suggestion is made is the image of ourselves gliding peacefully through the day, always in touch with the Spirit, carrying a joyous, grateful, prayerful presence with us in all our encounters and activities. I do not know about you, but this picture does not describe my daily life.

Work and family life bring pressure, conflict, worry, annoyance, and stress. People sometimes do not like what we have said or done, we run out of money, we allow too many demands to impinge on us at once, and so tiredness and reactivity set in. We are not always at our best. Obviously, life is not like that all the time, and there are times when we feel quite grounded in God as we go through our activities. But often enough, life is hard, and we do not feel very "spiritual."

If we carry a sense that the feelings we sometimes have on the cushion should always be with us through the day, we will not only feel disappointed; we will feel inadequate. We imagine that if we only just tried harder, perhaps we could "let go" of everything as it comes along, and dwell in greater harmony, love, and tranquility.

I do not think that this model is realistic or even helpful. It does not even fit the figures of holiness in scripture and the saints of our history. They were human, not angels. They struggled, fought, fell down, got up again, worried, cried, got angry, made mistakes, asked for forgiveness, and stumbled forward.

There is a way for us to be just as human as they were and also to develop a contemplative consciousness so that our lives become a prayer. It has to do with the principle that forms the foundation of prayer outlined in the first section of this book. We must, I believe, develop the capacity for self-awareness and worship in all that we do.

Self-awareness, practiced on the cushion, is the attention that we bring to the moment at hand, just as it is. This does not mean that we bring attention only to the breath, to the sounds and bodily sensations of the moment. It also means that we bring attention to whatever is arising in us in the way of thought-activity, emotional reaction, and the content of our "daydreaming." To become fully self-aware, we must experience ourselves as we are right now, no matter what it is. For this to be prayer, for it to be a transformative activity (and not just an exercise in navel-gazing), we hold this offering of the self in the moment before God, asking for the Spirit to do whatever needs to be done with it.

This also describes the practice of contemplative self-awareness in everyday life. For our lives to become more prayerful, we must bring the principle of honest and humble attention to all our activities. What this means is that we learn to mentally step outside our daydreams, outside the momentum of thought, emotion, and activity from time to time and observe what we are doing. As we find ourselves caught up in stress, we feel the body. As we argue with a co-worker, we notice the attachment. As we worry about the next thing coming along, notice what we are imagining and we feel the fear. As we daydream, we see the content of our mental wanderings. As a car cuts us off on the freeway, we feel the anger rising up. As someone challenges our plans, we notice the defensiveness as it emerges. As we jump into escapism, we pay attention to that which we are escaping from. In all that we do, we learn to bring self-awareness.

As we do so, we hold it before God as an offering of this moment, as an offering of who we are in this moment. We make this offering without trying to change it ("okay now I'm going to move myself from attachment to freedom, anger to love, worry to peace..."); without trying to understand it ("she said this, and that triggered me..."); without judgment ("How could I have done that? Why do I always keep doing that?"). We just experience where we really are, and humbly expose this to the Spirit.

This is a profoundly transformative way of living. When practiced on the cushion, it certainly does a lot of good. But when it moves outward into the moments of our days, it hits us where we live; it enters directly, in the moment, into our attachments, our blind habits, and our futile efforts to control. As we practice non-judgmental self-awareness in our life, we build a habit that gradually increases over time, to the point where unawareness becomes quite infrequent. The habit of prayerful attentiveness erodes our ability to go through life on auto-pilot; it breaks down our tendency to be jerked around by life's circumstances and our own reactivity. Self-awareness that takes place in the moment, as it is happening frees us from being a victim of life and our own unexamined habits of thought, emotion, and behavior.

The reason for this is that the Spirit honors our honesty and receives our offering. Because we make this offering in the sure knowledge that we have no power in ourselves to transform ourselves, in the understanding that we are dependent upon God to move us from where we are to where we need to be, the Spirit takes this humble offering of self and gradually works on us. It is the Spirit who changes us, who takes our fear, control, and attachment and turns it into love, freedom, and peace.

But prayer is not just self-awareness; it is also worship. Prayer is not just about us; it is about God. By the same token, our everyday consciousness is not just about what we are feeling and doing and how we find ourselves blocking the Spirit. It is about opening up to a reality beyond the self entirely, to the transcendent goodness of God.

In the broadest sense, worship is not just confined to those moments of intentional praise and adoration when we feel and express our devotion to God. It also includes all those moments when our hearts are open to the beauty and mystery of life, when the scales fall off our eyes and we just see the wonder and harmony of all that is. How do we sustain this through our day?

For me, it has to do with bringing a non-judging attention, again, to the moment. Only in this case, we bring this attention to the world around us, not just to ourselves. We bring awareness to other people as they are, seeing them with appreciative openness to who they are in this moment, without the need to evaluate, correct, or manipulate them. We see the sky, the earth; we smell the air; hear the rustling of leaves; and feel the breeze. We listen to the noise of the city and feel the turbine of its human activity. Without wishing we were somewhere else, or that life around us were different, we appreciate the world as it presents itself to us right now. This too is worship, for God is present in and through everything, everywhere.

To some extent we can make ourselves do this. We can decide that this is a good thing to do, and remember at times to just see, appreciate, and hear in gratitude. This is a habit that can be built through effort. But it is also the natural consequence of doing the same thing in our daily sessions of contemplative prayer. As we develop our capacities to sit quietly and feel our breath and see the quality of light in the room, as we open our hearts to God's fulsome presence in the emptiness of silence and stillness, we also develop our capacities to carry relative stillness and openness into our day. The more we practice this in prayer, the more we naturally find ourselves more open, grateful, attentive, and worshipful in our everyday consciousness, without effort or even intention.

What is the purpose of all this? Why is it important to bring self-awareness and worship into our daily lives? Is it just so that we can feel better? I hope not. While much of our contemporary culture defines "spirituality" as a kind of self-maintenance program (along with diet, exercise, and relaxation), the point of prayer is transformation so that we can then be more faithful, loving, and just in how we live. The point of integrating prayer into our daily experience is so that we can be more effective participants in building God's kingdom here on earth. The point of gratitude, peace, and honest self-awareness is so that we can get ourselves out of the way and be better agents of God's life for others who so desperately need it.

Summary

In order to go deeper in our life in God, we must apply ourselves differently, as the Spirit brings us into new territory. We must continue with perseverance when prayer becomes dull and we feel no rewards for doing so. We must remember our humanity, back off and trust in

God when we discover that we are pushing ahead too hard. When God seems distant, even absent, we must allow ourselves to move into unknowing, trusting that the God who loves us and for whom we yearn is found in emptiness and absence, too. When we feel like a spiritual failure, we must drop our expectations and learn to be humble beginners, neophytes in faith, not daring to "know" what we need or desire from God. Finally, we must eventually leave nothing out, so that we live every moment of our days in self-awareness and worship. Such is the contemplative journey, as it takes us more deeply, by grace, into God's life.

Eight

☙

Learning from Difficulty

I N MANY WAYS, MEDITATION is like a focused place, a
kind of workshop, where all the issues of life come in
and get special attention. Whatever is troubling us will
arise in silence. Our attachments, ambitions, and fears
will all come up. And most certainly, our relational and
circumstantial struggles will show up as well. Just like in
life, during the time of meditation we will experience
physical, emotional, and mental difficulties.

There is one important difference, however, between
experiencing difficulties in contemplation and during
our everyday lives. In the activity of our day we find
various ways of giving ourselves relief from struggle.
We go to a movie, we talk it out with a friend, we use
alcohol or caffeine, we do any number of things that will
temporarily change our perspective. In meditation that
is still and silent, we temporarily refrain from relief. We
do this in order to experience the difficulty more fully.
For contemplative prayer is not a way to replace our
difficulties with something more spiritually desirable; it
is a way of entering through the spiritual gate of
difficulty itself.

The awareness we bring to this effort is like a workshop
where specific, intensive work takes place in a way that it
cannot in our more diffused lives. And so in the still,
silent workshop of contemplation, our intentional and
focused attention allows us to slowly and quietly learn
something from our difficulties.

Remain Where You Are

Many forms of contemplative prayer do not require the meditator to sit still. When any discomfort arises, you simply shift around in your chair or cushion, stretch your legs, or change positions. The eyes are free to be open or closed, to wander around or to stay still. The time of prayer is not fixed, and when you feel that enough is enough, you simply get up. Posture is not considered important enough to teach, and it does not really matter whether you sit up or lean against a wall, take a walk or sit hunched over. During prayer it is not unusual to act on the impulse to pick up a book and read a short passage meditatively, in order to re-focus the thoughts.

There is nothing wrong with prayer that is practiced like this. For many years this was how I prayed, with much benefit. But there is something that this approach will never deal with effectively in a direct way during meditation: learning from the difficulty of meditation itself. But should prayer be comfortable, right? Life is hard enough; prayer should be a form of relief and refreshment from the difficulty of life, right? Why should meditation be hard work?

Because life itself is difficult. In life we are uncomfortable, bored, in pain. We suffer. Why should contemplation be any different? It is not that we seek to make ourselves suffer, but when these things arise in meditation, it may be more useful to stay present to them and learn from them, rather than turn away from them. At times in our daily lives we may not have the luxury of changing or getting away from difficulties. And so it can be useful to learn how to stay with whatever comes up, that our struggle may become our teacher. In contemplation, we focus and contain the difficulties of life, paying close attention, and giving ourselves opportunities to learn something about ourselves.

And so in the focused workshop of contemplative prayer we learn how to stay with something, often something simple, like an avalanche of confused thoughts, or a pain in the leg, until our resistance to it begins to melt. At this point the difficulty transforms, and also transforms us. With our resistance to difficulty out of the way, it is now free to become our teacher. Learning this in the focused workshop of meditation, we then take this out into daily life, and begin to approach our problems differently. Life then is not so much a never-quite-right situation that needs to be made better, or a series of problems to be solved, but rather something we can be present to, no matter what is going on. This attitude of presence changes us from within. Our difficulties may persist, but they no longer have the grip over us that they did before, because life is no longer defined by them. When a problem ceases to be a problem, it becomes our teacher. It becomes just another one of life's endlessly fascinating and unfolding realities.

In fact, opening to that which is can be a profoundly kind way of treating ourselves. There is a sort of subtle violence we do to ourselves when we constantly judge, worry, and plan; when we try our hardest to change our experience, alter our moods, and willfully force life into submission. It is much gentler and kinder to allow ourselves to be where we are, to settle into difficulty and let it be what it is. It can be a real relief to finally admit and experience what we have been unsuccessfully trying to run away from all along.

It must be remembered, however, that sitting through difficulty is not, in fact, productive for everyone at all times. Some are stuck at a point in their lives where they need conversation, therapy, medication, or a decisive change in their lives much more than they need to continue to experience their difficulty. Those who are attracted to Zen meditation or Christian contemplative prayer often hold out an ideal that it is always useful to stick it out and just experience whatever is going on. They think that there is an ironclad rule that it is always the spiritual thing to do to. In fact, sitting through difficulty may be the worst thing to do. Instead, we may need help from another person. We may need to take some sort of action or change of direction. This is why it is so important when practicing a demanding spiritual discipline to be under the direction of a teacher, a spiritual director, a therapist, or at least to be in conversation with friends who may have a different perspective.

But for many of us, learning to live with our difficulties is the beginning of real change. For we spend our lives trying to change things, to solve problems, to look somewhere else for the solutions to our problems. To put it mildly, our culture supports this kind of approach. And so for many of us, it is a new experience to sit still and learn from the reality of life as it is. The fact of the matter is, much of the time we cannot change our circumstances, no matter how we try. Whether we are simply experiencing the boredom of a job that we are not immediately able to change, or a nagging sense of anxiety that we have lived through for years and have even come to understand through therapy, sometimes we just cannot change our experience. This is when the practice of being present to our difficulty becomes especially useful.

The alternative to being with our problems, when they cannot be changed, is to make ourselves a little crazy. We push against something that will not move, or we just suffer the anxiety of non-acceptance, searching our minds and spinning our wheels trying, trying, trying, when nothing can be done. The task at this point is to learn from what is. This is what really transforms us into saints.

> One of the great spiritual tragedies is that so
> many people of good will would become persons

of noble soul, if only they would not panic and resolve the painful tensions within their lives too prematurely, but rather stay with them long enough, as one does in a dark night of the soul, until those tensions are transformed and help give birth to what is most noble inside of us— compassion, forgiveness, and love.

~ Jacques Maritain

Physical Stillness

What would a form of contemplative prayer look like, then, that seeks to learn from difficulty? It begins with an upright, alert posture. Sitting in a chair or on a cushion, the back is straight and tall without being tense. The eyes are slightly open and fixed on a spot on the wall or floor in front of you. The entire posture is one of alert relaxation and utter stillness. It is useful to watch this stillness carefully, to see if one is moving the eyes around just a little bit, shifting the toes, fingers, or even the tongue. The only thing that should be moving is the breath.

A specific time period for meditation should be set ahead of time, preferably with a timer, so that you sit for the complete time without moving, without having to look at a clock or think about when the allotted time will be up. The attitude should be one of commitment to the time, the place, the stillness, and the silence. If you are not committed to a period of time, there will always be a door open for you to exit prayer when things get hard. And so there should be no room for wiggling out of this commitment. Do not begin with too long a period. See what time frame "stretches your bow," without breaking it.

For some people, even reading this suggestion raises difficulties. Perhaps you feel resistance, anxiety, or rebelliousness. To actually do it inevitably raises even more difficulties. Sooner or later, over time you will feel boredom, physical pain, and emotional distress. Thoughts will multiply and speed up, crashing into one another in uncontrollable chaos. Your legs will fall asleep and ache. Time will stretch out impossibly, and you will be convinced that the battery in the timer has suddenly gone dead. You will get drowsy and maybe even drop off to sleep again and again during your allotted time. A hundred things will come to mind that you just have to do, and you will feel the seemingly irresistible urge to get up and do them (or at least write them down before you forget them). You will have an itch that you think you must scratch, or…or…something terrible will happen. You will find yourself feeling as if you must shift your position, in order to temporarily give yourself the illusion that you can find refreshment and change that way. You will feel unrestrained rage, and be confused as to where it's coming from, or you'll cry for no reason. Simply sitting still will allow life's difficulties to arise. Refraining from turning away from them will give you the opportunity to learn what they may have to teach you.

It is ridiculous, but quite common, to fantasize that everyone else has an easy time of it, and therefore to conclude that you should pretend that it is easy for you, too. Sitting in silence and stillness for lengthy periods of time is hard for everyone, and there is no way around this difficulty. Sooner or later, it gets hard for everyone in different ways, and that is a necessary and helpful part of the process.

Especially when beginning, remember that it takes time to find a physical position that allows one to remain alert and relaxed. Do not hurt yourself. Many Zen students have foolishly done permanent damage to their bodies by not listening to the warning signs. If pain becomes intense, there may be something wrong with the way you are sitting. Get advice from an experienced teacher. There is nothing less spiritual about using a chair or a kneeling bench if you are unable to sit cross-legged. Similarly, emotional or mental pain can become too much. If so, take care of yourself and get up, rather than harming yourself. Ultimately, only you and your teacher can discern that fine line between useful difficulty and pain that is destructive. Over time, you will know when you are shifting your posture or getting up from contemplation in order to avoid life's inevitable pain, and when you are doing so because you really should. Finally, some people are just not emotionally ready for silent meditation. It is a powerful tool, and sometimes other work such as therapy must be undertaken first.

God Stretches Us

One of the things that happens when we are able and willing to be with our difficulty is that it stretches us beyond where we think we can go. Again, this is not some sort of macho trip about endurance but rather the undoing of our assumptions about ourselves. What becomes stretched is our whole system of preferences, of likes and dislikes. Physical, mental, and emotional pain, distress and difficulty—much of this is simply the discomfort that arises when what we prefer has been threatened. Someone treats us in a way which we do not like; we unexpectedly lose money; illness strikes; or the weather changes in a way that disrupts what we prefer. This is inevitable, and because we hold tightly to our preferences, so is suffering. For suffering is the result of our preferences being violated.

When we sit still and allow the things we dislike to be, we stretch ourselves past our whole system of preferences and dislikes. To not do anything about those things that we usually try actively to change, is to disrupt our whole orientation about life being made up of good things and bad things. To respond neutrally to everything, no matter what it is, during the period of time allotted for meditation, is to radically question whether it makes any sense at all to have preferences. For over time, we learn that pain is just certain bodily sensations with thoughts and emotions surrounding it, and difficulty is just the violation of what we prefer. They are not good or bad, they just are. As Abba Nilus, one of the desert fathers advised:

> Do not be always wanting everything to turn out as you think it should, but rather as God pleases, then you will be undisturbed and thankful in your prayer.[1]

In fact, this advice is not only applicable to prayer; the desert fathers recognized that our preferences in life must be challenged continually in order to be able to embrace the will of God over our own wills. Again and again there are stories of self-denial, even to the point of putting themselves in a position of deliberately not getting what they wanted, for the sake of a higher good. They give away clothes, precious copies of the scriptures, positions of honor, food, anything that will humble them. Here is the voice of Abba Cronius, speaking of how God is born in us when we empty ourselves of the will:

> If the soul is vigilant and withdraws from all distraction and abandons its own will, then the spirit of God invades it and it can conceive because it is free to do so.[2]

When we are willing, in meditation, to sit through what we normally would not sit through, we are broken open to a different relationship to life. Giving up our wills, we make room for God's will. Acceptance and attention, rather than judgment and action, undermine our usual ways of relating and reacting to life. Slowly, the result is that we are more at peace with life, no matter

---

1 *The Sayings of the Desert Fathers*, Ward, 154.
2 *Ibid.*, 115.

what it may bring to us. We begin to understand what
St. Paul spoke about in the following passage:

> Rejoice in the Lord always. Again, I say, rejoice...
> I have learned the secret of being well-fed and
> of going hungry, of having plenty and of being
> in need. I can do all things through him who
> strengthens me.
> (Philippians 4:4, 12b–13)

Difficulty transformed

There is another transformation at work as we sit
with difficulty: our experience of difficulty itself will
inevitably transform. Life is continually evolving, and so
are we. When we wake up in the morning slightly "off,"
feeling kind of down, we discover by the afternoon that
the mood has curiously vanished for no apparent reason.
This is natural, and the more we can come to accept it,
the more we will be at peace with ourselves in whatever
circumstances.

During still, silent contemplation, the pain we feel may
be physical. Our back may be tired, our knees may ache,
or we just feel like we cannot maintain the upright
posture. As we stay with this, however, we begin to
discover what is actually taking place. We find that what
we call "pain" is actually a combination of physical
sensations and mental and emotional responses to those
sensations. In the body lies the actual content of pain. In
the mind lie thoughts about the pain: "This is awful...I
don't like it...when will it end?...oh, no, it's getting
worse...I shouldn't have to sit here like this, it is
pointless...." We may feel panic, fear, or anger. If we
observe ourselves and ask the question "What is this
pain?" we may be able to begin separating out what is
physical pain and what we are adding to it mentally and
emotionally.

At the point where we may be able to look past the mental distress and ask ourselves this question, we discover that the physical pain itself is simply a sensation of tightness or heat. If we bring awareness to the pain and to our thoughts and emotions surrounding it, we will find that the pain transforms from something terrible to something interesting. It may even go away once the added thoughts about it have been uncovered. We will also discover something about the nature of our reactions to pain.

During contemplation, there is another kind of difficulty, and that is mental. We simply cannot control our thoughts. Our minds seem to have a mind of their own. I do not know anyone who can stop his or her thinking for any great length of time. At times, our minds spin like some crazy, out-of-control fantasy machine. Every once in awhile we manage to get the thing in neutral, gasping in the silence for a moment before the machine puts itself in gear and takes off again. After many years of contemplation, it continues to amaze me just how relentless the false self is as it generates thought after thought, trying its hardest to control and make sense of life.

Our response to this relentless, uncontrollable mental activity might be despair, because we want not only to control our lives, we want to control our meditation. Even as the false self is spinning out thoughts to control life, it jumps into our practice and demands that we exert control over itself, that we stop it from doing what it is doing. It is almost as if the false self is at war with itself, creating havoc and then insisting that we use it to stop the havoc at the same time! But this is only because the ego is everywhere, even in our practice. The sad fact is that we cannot use the ego to control the ego.

There is another alternative to this egocentric effort to control our minds. And that is to watch patiently, to step out of the struggle to control entirely, to surrender.

Instead of trying to control what cannot be controlled by means of something that is part of the problem in the first place, we just watch what is happening. Through awareness, the mind naturally slows down. As we notice its games, its frantic efforts to manage everything, it begins to lose its unconscious power. It is as if the mental machine functions best in the darkness, and when we bring the light of awareness to it, it begins to lose its ability to function.

What also happens over time is that we begin to experience in a more active way the perspective of the observer, the true self, which is God's Spirit within us. This observing self is neutral, not charged with all of our usual attachments, efforts to control, and loaded meanings we associate with what is going on. It simply sees and accepts all with perfect clarity. Thus, watching our minds without judgment, we may even begin to ask the astonishing and unanswerable question "Who or what is doing the watching?" Even though we cannot find words to answer this question, we learn to know it; we recognize when we are in this neutral, accepting, clear, and free place. Over time, the strength and immediacy of this observer becomes more apparent and accessible.

Finally, meditation will bring yet another kind of difficulty, and that is emotional pain. Sitting in silence, we will not be able to escape the emotions that are present in our lives, and we should not try to escape them. They too need awareness. When we are temporarily depressed, depression will become intensely present in contemplation. When we are upset, we will be especially so in silence. Thoughts will be generated about our upsetting circumstances, and along with those thoughts will come emotional reactivity. The body will tense up around certain kinds of thoughts; it will react to what we are thinking. At times our emotions will become so intense in the still silence that they will seem unbearable; at times we will just start crying or laughing and not really know why. Perhaps by just allowing ourselves to be present and vulnerable for prolonged periods of time, we let down our defenses and distractions, thus giving permission and space to the emotions so that they can arise.

But again, attention brings transformation. By letting the emotions simply be there, they begin to evolve and simplify. At first, the emotion of anger may be surrounded by thoughts: "How can I protect myself, how can I show everyone how wrong she is? How can anyone do such a thing?" As we observe these egocentric thoughts in the container of observant awareness, they begin to drop away on their own. What is left is a clearer and purer emotion. Instead of outwardly-directed anger, we may discover sadness or raw fear. What is left is the pure and simple is-ness of the emotion, the wordless experience of reality that comes when we hit bottom and sit there silently, knowing it. At this point, most of our thoughts cease, because we have come to reality, and there is nothing left to think or say. It simply is.

This emotional transformation is profound. It truly changes us. Without analysis or interpretation, without trying to figure out the root of it all, we come to reality and reality heals us. We go away from this prayerful encounter a new man or woman. The emotion may come back again and again, but we have begun the process of undoing its power through awareness. It becomes easier each time to get to the bottom, because it is more and more familiar to us. Years ago when I was in therapy, the psychologist remarked that she felt that she had, in my contemplative practice, a partner therapist who was working with her. Indeed, the practice of presence and awareness brings something to emotional transformation that insight alone cannot touch.

And so whether our pain during meditation is physical, mental, or emotional, it will inevitably evolve, simplify, clarify, and lessen in its power as we bring it into the workshop of attention, where it gets exposed to the healing light of God's graceful truth. In a real sense, the kind of awareness I suggest here is nothing less than the judgment of God at work. It is the Spirit's eyes that we use when we see ourselves as we really are, with objective clarity and acceptance. And God's judgment is simply the truth about our sin and brokenness, offered in love so that we might be healed.

It is becoming clearer and clearer to me over the years that at the deepest level, we cannot change ourselves; but we can be changed. All we can do is bring trust and non-judgmental and thorough attention to our experience. That is all we can do. The rest is up to God, who with clarity and compassion contains everything we see. Transformation occurs as we allow our difficulties to be what they are—nothing more and nothing less—and offer them to God in humility. This is tremendously hard to do; it takes everything we have got. But we do not need to go the next step and try to get rid of or change our pain. All we must do is be patient in the workshop of contemplation. In the silence, something else, the relentless power of healing, wisdom, and life which we call God, is at work in a hidden way. Over and over again, we bring awareness to our lives; we turn around one day and notice that we have been changed. This is the hidden grace of God at work.

Redemptive Suffering

I do not believe that everything happens for a reason. I think that God created the world in such a way so that some things just happen. People get cancer. Water gets in a fuel line, the small plane stalls, and a family goes down. Avalanches, hurricanes, volcanoes, mudslides, and other "acts of God" are not acts of God at all, or even natural disasters permitted by God, but rather things that just happen in this world.

When suffering strikes, it can be disastrous. Many marriages eventually break up after the death of a child. Sickness can make a person lose faith in God. But suffering can also be redeemed, because while God doesn't make or even allow specific forms of suffering to strike us, God is always present through our pain. This presence changes our suffering into something else; it becomes not an evil force but a strange and unwelcome gift that brings, eventually, something good.

In the novel *Cold Mountain,* the hero, Charles Frazier, makes a long and horribly arduous journey home through a ruined South at the end of the Civil War. He contemplates turning himself in to the Union army, hoping that they will have compassion on him. His hope is based upon his perception that soldiers on both sides have suffered terribly, and that suffering makes people either bitter or it gives them compassion for others. I believe this to be true.

Years ago during seminary I spent a summer on a hospital ward as part of my pastoral training. I could go from one room to the next, a distance of no more than a few feet, and encounter a person with the exact same condition and prognosis as the person in the previous room. To my amazement, the first might be consumed in bitterness, asking why this had to happen to them, angry at this disastrous and unfair turn of events in their life. The second person might respond to the same exact same circumstance with grace, humor, faith, acceptance, and compassion for others. The first was ruined and the second was redeemed.

Suffering can be redemptive. It is not given to us in order to redeem us, but by its inevitable presence in our lives, we are given the opportunity to be changed for the better by it. The mother who loses a child will never say that this tragedy was a good thing, but she may gain from it freedom, compassion, devotion to God, passion for service to others, or clarity about her priorities. Gifts such as these would never have been possible for her without the event of suffering that turned her life upside down in the first place.

This is the mystery of the cross. Jesus, I believe, was not sent by the Father for the sole purpose of being killed as a payment for the debt of humanity's sin. This popular idea is sadistic in its view of God's demand for punishment. Jesus was executed. He was executed at a young age because he was a threat to the political, religious, and military powers. This is what happens to many prophets. It was a tragic and early death, just like the tragic deaths of Martin Luther King, Jr., or Archbishop Romero of El Salvador.

The mystery of this cross, this tragic and extreme form of suffering, is that God is still victorious, still at work in bringing good from evil. The resurrection showed the world for all time that nothing can block life, love, and the perseverance of the Spirit. Death and evil were defeated because a greater reality was unveiled. Christ's suffering and his death on the cross was redemptive because the resurrection showed the power of God. It is redemptive for us because when we see that paschal mystery, that passage through death to life, we know for ourselves that whatever comes our way, God is still victorious, life is still good. This makes it possible to embrace suffering with a different perspective than if we believe that good fortune and health are the only hope we have.

Some people are able to understand and embrace the mystery of redemptive suffering more easily than others. A child who grows up in a broken, violent, or emotionally hostile environment will have a harder time believing that God's ultimate victory can be trusted than the one who grows up in peace, tranquility, and unconditional love. So the learning of faith in suffering may be much harder for some than for others.

But still, it can be learned. Contemplative practice can shape our faith in ways that help us move through suffering with compassion, acceptance, and grace instead of bitterness and a sense of betrayal and injustice.

When we learn to sit through difficulty in prayer, we are undertaking a powerful lesson that prepares us for larger forms of suffering in life. If we learn to accept the ridiculous obsessions of our mind in meditation, we might be in a better position to learn how to accept chronic pain, if it comes to us. If we can learn to accept the discomfort of sitting through our anxiety when we really want to jump up screaming, we will be better prepared when we have to endure a hospital stay, or the terrible pain of grief and loss. Contemplative prayer is a training ground that can prepare us for suffering.

It should be remembered that not all suffering becomes redemptive through contemplative acceptance. Some forms of suffering must be fought, turned around, changed. Redemption can come through empowerment, when a woman takes action and gets out of an abusive environment. It can come when a neighborhood or a whole people rise up and say "enough!" to oppression and injustice.

Humility

Contemplation, our workshop of the soul, must include the seemingly simple task of staying with whatever is going on, even if it is suffering. What this simple task teaches us, however, is a profound lesson about life itself. Sitting again and again within the contained and highly intensified workshop of difficulty, we discover that we are more likely then to do the same throughout our day. Patience grows as we learn to let life be what it is. Naturally, there will be times when we must act to change life, but much of the time we seek change not because something really needs changing, but rather because we are uncomfortable with it. Being with whatever comes up in contemplation allows us to be more at home in life, however it may present itself to us. This is what is behind the traditional Christian concept of suffering all things as the will of God. Now this attitude can certainly be one of passivity and blind acceptance of things that should, for the sake of justice and emotional health, not be accepted. Self-centered "martyrs" suffer everything quietly and resentfully, assuming that God mysteriously (and sadistically?) desires constant pain as some sort of punishment or discipline. But this view is a distortion. Another way of understanding that everything is the will of God is to say that life will be what it will be, and we cannot always control it. Much of what life presents us with is something that we would like to change or get away from, but cannot. In this case, our alternatives are to either fight against life in some kind of internal, unhappy and futile struggle, or to embrace what the moment brings and learn from it.

Sometimes the desert fathers put themselves in the position of suffering physically or emotionally, because they recognized that it would push them closer to trust in God and not in the circumstances of life. They undertook great physical privations towards this end, but sometimes their self-imposed trials were more of an emotional nature, chipping away even at the sense of self. Abba Isaiah said:

> Nothing is so useful to the beginner as insults.
> The beginner who bears insults is like a tree that
> is watered every day. [3]

In a story from the desert that is exactly parallel to a Zen story from another century, Macarius is slandered and accused by a young village girl of having impregnated

---

3 *Ibid.*, 69.

her. He accepts this false accusation with humility, embracing the suffering. In fact, he goes to his servant and tells him to sell his only possessions, a few baskets, so that he could give "his wife" something to eat. He worked day and night to provide for this slanderer, and when it came time for her to give birth, she had extreme difficulty in labor. But she finally confessed her lie, and the baby was born safely. The young girl and the villagers who believed her, of course, were humbled before the monk.[4]

While we may not go to such extremes, daily life gives us plenty of opportunity to bear small injustices and slander silently, to accept these small sufferings as a way to learn humility. Instead of protecting ourselves all the time against whatever we think might harm us or our reputation, sometimes it is best to learn from the suffering itself. And, of course, life will hand us our share of more intense forms of suffering as well. We should always do what we can to alleviate our own, or others', suffering, but when we cannot do so, our only alternative may be to accept and learn from it.

Humility is, for all the great teachers in the contemplative tradition, absolutely essential to the life of prayer and transformation, and a sure sign of the work of the Spirit. It is not only that suffering that brings humility, for in suffering we know that we cannot control what happens to us, but it gives us also a clear awareness of our sinful tendencies. Humility is also brought about simply by the impossible difficulty of sitting repeatedly in silent prayer. Whoever thinks that they are "good" at prayer, and a "spiritual" person, will soon have those illusions dashed after a little while in silence! It is a humbling experience indeed to discover that we cannot control our mind, we cannot "reach" God by deciding to do so, and we cannot remain "pure."

---

4 *Ibid.*, 124.

And so humility is essential to a life of prayer and spiritual transformation by grace. Amma Theodora told the following story:

> There was an anchorite who was able to banish the demons; and he asked them, "What makes you go away? Is it fasting?" They replied, "We do not eat or drink." "Is it vigils?" They replied, "We do not sleep." "Is it separation from the world?" "We live in the deserts." "What power sends you away then?" They said, "Nothing can overcome us, but only humility." Do you see how humility is victorious over the demons?[5]

Humility is essential precisely because it consists of the movement from complete self-reliance to dependence upon God and the grace of the Spirit within. Gradually in the relational context of contemplative prayer, we learn to trust God. We learn to trust that if we humbly stay with what we are experiencing within the container of God's presence, God will enlighten, guides and heal us. Everything will eventually be used by God for growth in the Spirit. Our work is to open up with awareness; it is God's work to use and transform what we experience. Over time we find that this process can be counted upon. With this learned trust and humility, we need not fear the difficulties of life, for all will be used for the life-directed purposes of God. Even suffering, when experienced and transformed in the workshop of awareness and grace, is part of goodness.

While God does not cause everything, God is in everything, even suffering. The grace of patience is more than just learning to grit our teeth and endure things. It is a radical, nonsensical opening to that which everything in us tells us to fight or avoid. It is the vulnerable embrace of life in all its richness, including

---

5 *Ibid.*, 84.

unavoidable difficulty. It is the transformation of what we thought was our enemy into our friend.

In this way, life shifts from being a war between good and evil to a "formless field of benefaction," as the Zen saying goes. All is included in the loving goodness of God. As Julian of Norwich said, "you will see yourself that every kind of thing will be well...it is God's will that we should know in general that all will be well."[6] Through the discipline of sitting still in meditation through whatever may emerge, we learn the grace of patience. And through patience we are transformed to see God in all, to know the reality that eventually rejoices even in suffering. For in God, nothing is wasted.

Summary

Becoming Christ includes an embrace of the cross. Jesus' path must become ours, and his path includes the cross. After all, Jesus spoke frequently of his own suffering and death that would come as an essential part of his journey. When Peter tried to deny this fact, Jesus rebuked him, even calling this denial demonic: "Get behind me, Satan! For you are setting your mind not on divine things but on human things"(Mark 8:33). Jesus then extended his cross into the lives of his followers: "If any want to become my followers, let them deny themselves and take up their cross." Just after he said this, he was transfigured in glory on the mountain top, in the presence of Peter and James and John. In this series of sayings and story, glory is related somehow to suffering, and Jesus will not let others deny this reality. Not only that, he teaches them that their own spiritual transfiguration will somehow involve suffering (Mark 9).

---

6 *Julian of Norwich: Showings*, trans. Edmund College, O.S.A. and James Walsh, S.J. (New York: Paulist, 1978), 232.

In our day there is a kind of popular spirituality that denies the cross, that runs away from darkness and difficulty instead of embracing it as part of our journey into holiness. This spiritual positivism claims that we can experience joy and enlightenment by getting rid of anything "negative," and by focusing on the "positive." While endemic to new age spiritualities, spiritual positivism is not limited to them. A tendency in this direction is found in the church as well. This is why we had to move the liturgical celebration of Good Friday, with its sober reading of the Passion Narrative, to Palm Sunday: in order to "catch" the worshipers on Sunday who would otherwise avoid Good Friday, thus skipping directly from the Hosanna! of Jesus' triumphal entry into Jerusalem to the Alleluia! of the resurrection.

For some, there is a benefit to the practice of positive thinking, and it is certainly human to try to avoid suffering. But I am afraid that Jesus would respond to spiritual positivism that denies the cross by saying that its followers have set their minds not on divine things, but on human things. For the path that leads to God leads through the cross, at some point.

A practice of contemplative prayer brings us to the cross. Certainly life will do the same, but in contemplative prayer we are given a way of working with the cross. The difficulties of our lives will arise in silence with God, and God will not magically fix or take them away. We must learn patience and humility, sitting through our pain with an open heart. We must learn to just be present to God with our difficulties. Instead of closing down around them, we open it up in love and adoration, in complete trust and vulnerability. By doing so, our pain is joined to God, and it is redeemed. We are transformed. Our suffering is no longer just "ours," a private possession: it is part of the pain of the world, part of the cross. Gazing at the cross, our private suffering is lifted up into Christ, who shares it and thus helps us transcend our prison of pain. But even more than that, Christ redeems our suffering, moving us into resurrection, so that we are made new people in him.

Nine

❈

Becoming Free

ONCE IN AWHILE I HAVE THE OPPORTUNITY to fly out of an area that is covered over by low clouds and rain. On the ground, things are dark, wet, windy, and cold. The mood of the weather surrounds me as I prepare to leave town, drive on city streets, arrive at the airport, get out of the car, and haul baggage around. I feel the storm inside and out. It seems that this is all there is, because it is all that I can see. "It is stormy," I say to myself. We get into the jet, watching the ground crew splashing around in their rain gear, and wondering what it must be like to have to work outdoors on such a day. The aircraft taxis down the runway and shudders a bit as it leaves the ground. A few of the passengers close their eyes and anxiously grip their armrests. We enter the clouds and all is obscured. Then, all of a sudden we lift out of the storm and everything is blue, clear, sunny, and calm. Below us is a blanket of clouds, like an enormous pillow of snow.

What is amazing to me is that every time this happens, I am surprised. On the ground I am a part of the storm. I think "It is stormy," and so I am stormy too, along with everything and everyone around me. Then all of a sudden, as we go above the storm the weather changes and so do I. Everything opens up. The surprise is not only the suddenness of the weather mood inside and out. It is also the realization that all along, the storm in which I was so caught up turned out to be small and was surrounded, only a few thousand feet up, by infinite miles of blue, clear, open, sunny sky. My perspective now includes both the storm on the ground and the sky above it. I am no longer just stormy, wet, small, and closed-in; I am still that, but I am also the wide expanse of clear sky. What surprises me is that when I was on the ground, I had no awareness whatsoever of the bigger picture that I now see.

Most of our lives are spent within the small perspective of ever-changing, all-consuming mental/emotional weather systems on the ground. On any given day, we temporarily feel depressed, hopeful, upset, gripped by desire or ambition, desperate, confused, happy, in love, lonely, etc. When we are feeling this, we really think that this is all there is. We are the temporary mood or state of awareness; we are happy, sad, angry, empty. Unknowingly, without even choosing to do so, we have identified with the mental/emotional weather that we are temporarily experiencing. To identify with any temporary state is to be gripped by it, to become its slave as it takes us where it wants us to go. We not only feel the anger, we are anger itself. We believe the anger, allowing it to direct our thoughts and actions in habitual ways. And so because we are anger, it takes us into gossip, revenge, control, escape, victim-hood, self-defense, or depression. We scramble to do something in response to the anger, unable to see anything other than what makes us mad. We are caught up in the temporary emotional weather system, unable to see outside of it.

I remember years ago when one of my sons was about three years old. He was sitting in the back seat of the car as I drove. A particularly cool car drove by, which caught his eye. He quietly said to himself "I am that car." He was so identified with what he thought was cool, with what he wanted, that he saw himself as that coolness, that desire. He became the object of his mental/emotional focus. We are no different. Wanting a project at work to be successful, we become that project, and we think we are its success or failure, at least temporarily. We become its slave, following it where it will take us.

All of this arises out of the mistaken belief that what we are thinking or feeling is real, that it has some kind of substance about it. Like the traveler on the ground, we believe that the storm is the way things are: we are anger, depression, confusion. We believe that it is something which has come upon us or which we have created, and as a thing we also believe that it has some kind of permanence. Our thoughts around the storm are also a part of this illusory substance. We believe our thoughts about it: "So and so caused this problem, they should not have done it; I am always like this, creating no good; there is something wrong with me,"...etc. We believe these interpretive thoughts, as if they are real. Joko Beck once said that we are all, relatively speaking, mentally ill, for anyone who believes her or his thoughts is mentally ill.

We are Not the Storm

Gregory of Nyssa, in sermon entitled, "Know Thyself," spoke of the necessity of being a guardian of our true self in Christ, that is, guarding what is real so that we might live out of reality instead of delusion. In this sense he echoes the desert practice of "guarding the heart" by "watching the mind" and all its intrigues. He speaks of the delusions of power, wealth, and beauty, but the same could be said about believing in the delusions of anger, confusion, suffering, and poor self-image.

> Our greatest protection is self-knowledge, and to
> avoid the delusion that we are seeing ourselves
> when we are in reality looking at something else.
> This is what happens to those who do not
> scrutinize themselves. What they see is strength,
> beauty, reputation, political power, abundant
> wealth, pomp, self-importance, bodily stature,

a certain grace of form or the like, and they think that this is what they are. Such persons make very poor guardians of themselves; because of their absorption in something else, they overlook what is their own and leave it unguarded.[1]

It is our false beliefs about ourselves that create suffering. Let us say an automatic gas shutoff in an old heater in a house gives out one day, and the heater blows up. Fortunately, no one is hurt, but there is some serious damage to the house. This temporary storm now has become some sort of thing with a sense of reality and permanence, because of our thoughts that surround the event: "I should have had it checked out at the beginning of the season, how could I have been such an idiot, we came within an inch of death, life is so uncertain and fragile, I can't afford to fix it, there goes my meager savings which were meant for a much needed vacation, now my work-related stress will get no relief, what else is now going to go wrong?"...and on and on. The temporary storm has now turned into some kind of presence that seems real, by which we are now controlled.

In fact, what has happened is that some gas ignited, causing a little fire and smoke damage, there was a big noise, and an appliance that used to work no longer does. Everything else is interpretation and belief. Without the accompanying thoughts, it is just a passing event that happened. Life will go on. The dog is temporarily distracted by the noise, and goes back to chewing on a bone. The crows outside are surprised and fly from one tree to another, continuing their squawking. We are still just who we are in God. But because of our thoughts and false beliefs, we now are

---

1 *From Glory to Glory: texts from Gregory of Nyssa's mystical writings*, selected by Jean Danielou, S.J., trans. and ed. Herbert Musurillo, S.J. (Crestwood NY: St. Vladimir's Seminary Press, 1979), 159.

filled with a dark presence, sure of its permanence, its meaning, its threatening reality.

This is how we live most of our lives, reacting to its temporary storms as if they are real and full of either danger or promise. What we are doing in this little drama is creating an illusory world that is parallel to what is actually happening. We are constructing an invisible but very powerful substitute reality on top of reality itself. We think that our temporary circumstances, our states of mind and emotion, or our thoughts about all of these things are real.

If we have some degree of self-awareness, we may come to realize at this point what we are doing. We see the anger or the boredom that we feel is possessing us, and we then try to change the mood. If we think that the mood is not good, we try to get ourselves out of it. Using the metaphor of the weather again, we realize that the storm is bad and that we should rise above it to the clear sunny sky, which is good. We have shifted from one self-identification to another, trying to change the weather. We may try to "let go," whatever that means, or to think positive thoughts, or to understand exactly what went "wrong" and who is to blame for our anger. In one way or another, we try to change the weather. And we do this because we have decided, again without even thinking about it, that one state is good and another is bad.

Living in sunny New Mexico, my wife and I tend to enjoy any change of weather, because it comes so infrequently. Sometimes we wake up, look at the blue sky, and mutter "Another damn sunny day." And so when it gets windy, or clouds envelop us, or once in a great while when it actually snows or rains, we are ecstatic. We build a fire, get out a book, make tea, and cherish the change. But we are surrounded by those who have grown up here, knowing practically nothing but sunny days, or those who have moved here from somewhere like Minnesota, who dread even the suggestion of what they have left behind. It seems that everyone panics when different weather comes. A little sleet falls, the roads ice over for a few hours, a car or two overturn, and the headlines scream MONSTER STORM RIPS THE STATE. The meteorologist describes the weather as "nasty, icky, yucky," and predicts that in a day or two "good" weather will return. And this is not just in New Mexico. It is almost a universal thing to hear people describe sunny warm weather as "good" and cold wet weather as "bad."

It is the same with our mental/emotional weather systems. We not only identify with our temporary moods, thinking that we are these moods, we make the further determination that it is good or bad. A "good" mental/emotional state is open, awake, peaceful, happy, simple, and loving. A "bad" state of mind is cloudy, dark, hopeless, complicated, and confused. If it is good, we do what we can to hold on to the mood. If it is bad, we try to get rid of it or get away from it. Whole schools of spirituality and psychology are dedicated to effective ways of changing the weather, so that we can move ourselves from bad states to good ones. It is commonly assumed that this is what religion or therapy is for: to help us feel those things we have always associated with the word "positive" and to be able not to feel those things that we have always associated with the word "negative."

There are several problems with this approach. The first is that whatever changes we manage to make, the "bad" weather will always come back. There is no escape for us, as human beings, from the temporary dark storms that will blow through our lives from time to time. We will never be able to stay in sunny, "ideal" weather all the time, and if our intention is to do so, there will always be some degree of frustration or sense of not being quite there yet, not quite permanently clear and happy. Another problem is that no method of emotional weather-changing really works, because all we are doing is substituting one ego-centered reaction (being caught up in a mood or an idea) for another (willfully trying to make ourselves be a certain way). We are still reacting to life as it comes to us, rather than appreciating it. And so even though we may try to rise above the storm, we are only continuing to be controlled by it.

The Spacious View

Our circumstances and our states of mind and emotion are just like the weather; they come and go, and then come again. We are not any thing at any given time, for we are constantly changing, just like the atmosphere and ecological environment of the earth. Everything is moving, evolving. Confusion gives way to clarity, ambitious hopefulness gives way to despair, heaviness gives way to light-heartedness. Watching the changes of our mental and emotional lives is like watching the weather.

Also like the weather, our temporary states are not all that there is at any given time. There is always the bigger picture, there is always blue clear sky surrounding the storm. Contemplation helps us to see everything: to be aware of the storm even as we also see the sky above it. The point of contemplation is not to help us rise above the storm so that we can get from a bad place to a good one. Its purpose is rather to help us see everything: the storm, the earth, the blue sky, and the infinity of space beyond. Its purpose is to see ourselves within the widest perspective possible: the perspective of God.

This wider perspective helps us not to be so identified with whatever temporary state we are in, and to learn to appreciate it, whatever it may be, as we might appreciate a good storm. What is so bad about feeling temporarily angry or depressed, especially if we see it from the wider perspective of God, rather than being caught up in it? Why do we have to get away from it, or change it? Eventually it is going to change anyway, as we watch it.

Of course, there are times when it is appropriate and necessary to change the weather. If we live in the north, we intentionally take vacations so that we can soak up some much-needed sun. If we are chronically depressed or angry, we undergo therapy or take medication for awhile in order to get ourselves out of whatever we are locked into. Instead of sitting there appreciating our headache, we take an aspirin. Instead of simply watching someone abuse us and others, we do something about it to change it.

But intentional change has its limits, and we forget this. Most of the time we cannot do anything about what we are temporarily experiencing. We are just bored or anxious or in an uncomfortable situation that we do not like for awhile, and we have to get through it. Seeing that the vast majority of our waking state falls into this category, rather than something that we can or should actually change, it becomes helpful to question our constant tendency to either identify with or attempt to change the temporary states in which we find ourselves. Much of the time it is appropriate to dis-identify and to question our judgments about what is good and what is bad. Contemplation helps us to do this.

When we sit in silence and observe whatever is going on within and around us, whether formally or in the course of our day, we make a subtle but important shift: we observe the phenomenon from a somewhat detached perspective, rather than seeing everything from within it. Sitting in silence, as a gripping concern arises, we watch the thoughts and bodily tensions that accompany this concern. Watching what is going on, we are like an outside observer who sees what is happening. Watching ourselves, we are also aware of sitting in God's presence. We may feel the storm of our personal drama, but we also have a view beyond it into the infinite goodness and clarity of God.

Because we are looking at ourselves from a more detached perspective, we are not the slave of what we experience. Whatever is going on is merely something that is temporarily passing through us, and the observer, or the true self in God, is witnessing it as it passes through our consciousness. Since the true self in God is unchangeable, unconditionally accepting, and at peace, the gripping concern is seen within the clear blue sky of awareness. We may feel the storm, but we are also experiencing the bigger picture which includes the calm. We are not making an egocentric effort to rise above the storm into the clarity of peace, but rather we are saying "Yes" to the storm as it runs its course, even as our peripheral vision includes God's presence. Our perspective in contemplation moves from being caught up in the storm to seeing everything at once.

This perspective is, I think, what Meister Eckhart (thirteenth-fourteenth century) was describing when he said :

> The eye by which I see God is the same as the
> eye by which God sees me. My eye and God's
> eye are one and the same—one in seeing,
> one in knowing, and one in loving.
> ~ from the sermon "Distinctions are lost in God"[2]

The observer who sees and embraces all is not only our true self, but God's Spirit within us. Our ability to see with unconditional acceptance and peace is nothing less than God's Spirit seeing through our eyes. Our true nature and God's nature are one. And so contemplation does not remove us from undesirable states of mind or emotion; it broadens our perspective so that whatever is going on is seen with the divine eye of the Spirit within, and all is known to be contained in the infinite peace

---

2 *Meister Eckhart: a Modern Translation*, trans. Raymond B. Blakney (New York: Harper and Row 1941) 206.

and clarity of God. In fact, according to Gregory of Nyssa, our ability to see things in the wider perspective changes us, so that we become larger in the life of contemplative grace:

> Participation in the divine good is such that, where it occurs, it makes the participant ever greater and more spacious than before, bringing to it an increase in size and strength, in such wise that the participant, nourished in this way, never stops growing and keeps getting larger and larger.[3]

When I am sitting in meditation, or when I come to awareness in the course of my day, sometimes a storm suddenly comes up. Like a summer squall on a lake, darkness, wind, and rain pour into my windows, seemingly from nowhere. I am, without warning, afraid and feeling reactive. When I manage to dis-identify with this state and resist the impulse to react, I drop down into the moment, finding stillness in the midst of the storm. The storm rages on, but I am now watching it rather than identifying with it or running away from it. It is as if I am sitting in my house and listening carefully to the crashing sounds and feeling the rushing winds. Because I am watching from within my house (the perspective of the Spirit within), because God is watching through me, the storm becomes exciting and intense, rather than some kind of threat. My fear dissolves into wakefulness. The storm is experienced within the bigger perspective of the clear sky around it.

At first, in our contemplative practice we will only be able to move in and out of this perspective. We will go back and forth between being gripped by our concern and seeing it from the wider perspective. In the silence of meditation, we will find ourselves caught up in

---

3 *Glory to Glory*, Danielou, Musurillo, 62.

worrisome thoughts for some minutes, then suddenly step back and notice where we have been, now seeing it from the point of view of the observer. For a moment we may feel calm and clear, then find ourselves plunged back again into the storm. Back and forth we go, from being caught up to being the more free observer. This is a good beginning.

But eventually we learn to experience both at the same time. We learn to sit still in meditation and to allow the storm, and even as we see and feel it, we also see and feel the clear sky of awareness around it. We learn to be aware of the drama of the self, even as we are aware of God. Even as we are facing someone who is angry with us and as we watch the internal tension and rising impulse to react, we also can see what we are doing. We are able to contain it within the bigger picture, rather than become it in all its smallness. We are not getting rid of anything; in fact, we are adding something to our temporary storm. We are adding everything else around it. We are remembering God.

Thomas Kelly (1893–1941) was a Quaker who understood this development in the life of prayer. He knew that at first we must go back and forth between unawareness and awareness, moving from being caught up in the circumstances and concerns of our lives to a more open and clear space of prayerfulness. But eventually the life of prayer will bring with it an ability to be open to both at once.

> At first the practice of inward prayer is a process of alternation of attention between outer things and the Inner Light. Preoccupation with either brings the loss of the other. Yet what is sought is not alternation, but simultaneity, worship undergirding every moment, living prayer, the continuous current and background of all moments of life. Long practice indeed is needed

before alternation yields to concurrent immersion
in both levels at once.

~ *Testament of Devotion,* 38–40[4]

It is this simultaneity that contemplation brings: being
aware of whatever is going on and, at the same time,
seeing it from a wider perspective. In order to practice
doing this, let me suggest the following exercise.

Begin your time of prayer by paying close attention
only to your breath for a few moments. Hold this
awareness of breath as you feel the balance of your body.
Notice your posture, your overall position. Holding this
background awareness of breath and balance, move your
awareness through your senses. With your eyes open and
fixed on a point in front of you, see everything,
including what is within your peripheral vision. Smell
whatever odors are around, and taste your mouth. Listen
to the subtle sounds within and around you. Try to
maintain an open awareness that includes more than
one part of this overall picture at once. Your attention
will alternate between breath and hearing, posture and
sight. But try to hold more than one aspect together in
your consciousness at the same time. Maintain an
overall sense of your physical, sensory state. Remember
that this being present to the moment is a way of being
present to God, who is this very moment. With your
eyes open to life in this moment and your heart open to
God, maintain yourself this way for a few moments.

As thoughts arise, and they will, let them be there,
observing them from the perspective of your physical,
sensory state. Continue to feel the sensory reality of this
moment in God even as you watch your thoughts or
emotions. You will notice that you alternate between
being caught up in your concerns and paying attention
to the fact of the moment in God. But rather than trying

---

4 *Quaker Spirituality: Selected Writings,* ed. Douglas V. Steere
(Mahwah, NJ: Paulist 1984), 292.

to get rid of the concerns that arise, try to pull back from them just a little bit so that they are included within the wider perspective of physical awareness in the pure stillness of the moment in God.

This will be difficult at first. Perhaps it is not even possible for you to try to do it right now. Perhaps instead it will come as one of the fruits of contemplation. Eventually, you will find yourself sitting with some gripping concern, but instead of being enslaved and manipulated by it, you will see it from within the place of unconditional acceptance and the presence of God. Your concern will come and go like a brief storm on the face of the earth, while the sky above continues in its clear presence. This is your eye and God's eye as one seeing, allowing your life and the world to be what it is, simultaneously knowing it to be within the infinitely wide container of eternity.

Detachment

The early contemplative fathers of our tradition developed this spacious way of seeing all without judgment, accepting whatever came in life as part of the tapestry of existence. They would intentionally put themselves in situations where they knew that their attachments would be challenged, and where they would learn to take on the wider perspective of life in God. Such radical practices loosen the grip that is clenched around the way we want life to be, and allow for a movement into a greater freedom of spirit.

This spacious, freedom of spirit was called, in the desert tradition, *apatheia*. Despite this Greek word's obvious connection with the word apathy, contemplative *apatheia* is anything but apathetic. While some may believe the stereotype of the contemplative as a self-absorbed, uncaring and unfeeling person removed from the passions of life, and some contemplatives may fit this description, it is a false stereotype. Contemplative detachment, true *apatheia*, leads to a spacious view of life as God sees it, which leads to freedom and love. For the contemplative, detachment is freedom from attachments, not a distancing from people and from life. Detachment is liberty from the prison of all that enslaves us and keeps us from engaging in life with joy, peace, clarity, and love.

All of us struggle with attachments: how we think we are supposed to be, look, or feel; possessions; being liked; being a "winner" or even a "loser"; having a certain lifestyle; particular beliefs about others; and even the smallest, most insignificant details working out the way we want them to (like getting through an intersection before the light turns red). As long as we live, we will always, to some degree, be attached, at least from time to time. Such is the human condition. Detachment is the process of de-attaching. It is not the process of becoming an unfeeling automaton; it is de-attaching from the things that enslave us. As a contemporary commentator on the desert fathers noted:

> Apatheia destroys the attachment to "passions,"
> but these refer not to the God-given emotions…
> but rather to sinful, inner attachments to
> selfishness, rooted by sin in the natural
> passions. The sign of having attained this state
> of integration on the body, soul, and spirit levels
> is when the Christian can occupy his or her
> mind and heart with the continual presence
> of God.[5]

This integration, this liberty of spirit is *apatheia*, which frees us from everything that stands in the way of our enjoyment of life, of God, and of others. The path to this detachment is, I believe, feeling and observing our true

---

5 George Maloney, in the footnotes for *Pseudo-Macarius*, 286.

attachments in the moment, especially in silent prayer, then learning how to dis-identify with whatever has captured us, and moving into a place of seeing our attachments within the context of whole picture.

This spacious, big picture, which includes our human attachments but also the beauty and truth of life within and around them, is the divine perspective, a gift of the Spirit. It is seeing with God's eyes. This spacious perspective gives us the ability to be free and present to God in ways that are impossible when we are caught up in our attachments instead. Spacious detachment, *apatheia*, moves us out of our illusions and brings us back to reality, back to our true selves. Two contemplative fathers put it this way:

> When the intellect is no longer dissipated among external things or dispersed across the world through the senses, it returns to itself; and by means of itself it ascends to the thought of God.
> ~ Basil the Great

> The one who has *apatheia* has returned to himself, has entered into the treasure house that is within.
> ~ Isaac the Syrian

Returning to ourselves, we are able to be the person that we actually are in Christ. We are able, at least at times, to experience freedom from sin, suffering, and all the things in life that temporarily possess us.

Freedom to Love

If detachment is really of God, it must result in love. God is love, and any who live in God live in love. Love is always the test of who we are becoming in our spirituality. If we find ourselves more in love with God and life, if we find ourselves more able to love others unconditionally and joyfully, we can be certain that our spirituality is moving us God-ward. If we find ourselves moving into isolation, superiority, judgment of others, we are moving, in spite of our spirituality, or because of it, away from God.

The connection between detachment and love is this: if we learn to be free from the things that keep us enslaved, that keep us from being fully alive in the moment, then we will be able to be present to others in a way that is truly loving, truly free from our own baggage. The more we become aware of and free from our false self, the more our true self, which is Christ, arises within us. It is not a matter of trying to be more loving: it is a matter of Christ loving through us as our attachments cease.

It is a beginning stage in the Christian life to concern oneself with practicing virtue, with the effort to be a better person. This effort is the positive process of adding behavior and attitudes of goodness, through a combination of the exercise of our own will and God's grace. But the practice of virtue, while always a part of the human journey into God and therefore never complete, is not all there is. There is also the process of subtraction, of dying to the false self, where, through a combination of awareness and grace, we lose our attachments, our habitually destructive ways of being.

In this subtractive process, becoming a better person is not a matter of replacing destructive patterns with positive ones. For when we die to the false self, it is not up to us, through our own efforts, to resurrect ourselves into a new manner of being. Resurrection is God's work, not ours. When we subtract the false self, the new person comes into being by grace.

This is nothing less than the emergence of Christ resurrecting within us. It is not as if by dying to the false self we then build up a better "me." When we die spiritually, when our attachments are subtracted through awareness and grace, what is left is Christ. Our true nature is Christ, and instead of becoming a new "me," we become Christ, or more accurately, Christ becomes us. Christ is what is left when we subtract the false self. Dying to self is not a matter of merging into a shapeless divine void: it is a matter of getting out of the way so that the specific character of the resurrected Christ may emerge from its previously blocked position within.

This specific character, which is the resurrected Christ, is love. Just as Jesus embodied love in his lifetime, healing, forgiving, and freeing others, he embodies love in us when he arises within. We are free to love as Christ loves through us, because the baggage of the false self is sufficiently out of the way.

There is a concrete way in which we can see the attachment to our own baggage at work in our relationships. When we are attached, we are concerned about ourselves. We listen to another, waiting for them to finish what they are saying so that we can make our point, end up looking good, or convince them of the legitimacy of our point of view. When someone says something that is unkind, we react protectively, defensively, in the hopes that we will push the hurt away. When someone does something that threatens the way we want things to turn out, we scramble mentally in order to figure out how to jockey for a more advantageous position.

It is not that these behaviors are always wrong, because sometimes we do have to be wise as serpents; there can be times when we have to argue, defend, push things away, and jockey for position. It is just that when we do these things out of a position of self-centered attachment rather than out of clarity, love, freedom, and peace, we will always be destructive.

Let us say that someone really pushes our buttons, and we find ourselves all stirred up. This is the moment to take a break, breathe deeply, and look within. Paying scrupulous attention to our thoughts and emotions, we will discover, eventually, our attachments. We will discover that our reactive mode is not at all clear, free, and loving; it is afraid, defensive, and self-serving. Bringing these attachments to awareness, we feel them fully and offer them to God. Eventually, the attachment dies, for the moment, and what is left is clarity and love.

This is because rather than reacting automatically, or even trying to be good in spite of our attachment, as if we were putting a layer of virtue on top of the false self, we simply stop, feel, and die. We subtract, through awareness and grace, our baggage. What is left is our true nature, Christ resurrecting within. What is left is love. We become nothing, so that Christ can become everything in us.

At this point, we can move into action with clarity and with a true regard for the best for all concerned. We still might argue, push, or defend, but we do so not because we are driven by self-centeredness, but because we are compelled by love and truth. There is a great difference between loving action that is born out of detachment and action that is born out of attachment. When we are free, we are able to see ourselves and others in the best light, which is in the light of Christ. We see the other not as they appear to be, in a human light (attached and self-serving), but as they *are*, in a divine light, as Christ incarnate. This changes the relationship profoundly. We can now love unconditionally, freely, because we see ourselves and the other as Christ.

Normally we love ourselves and others because "the good outweighs the bad." We take stock of ourselves and others, acknowledging the faults and sins as well as the virtues and positive qualities of our personalites. If the balance tips towards the good, we like ourselves, we like others. This is, of course, normal and human.

But the spiritual view of ourselves and others is radically different. It is grounded instead in unconditional love, love that is not conditioned upon the human scale of good and bad. It is unconditional in that it views self and other as God views us: as Christ incarnate again. While this vision is never perfect or constant, from time to time we are able, with the freedom of detachment, to subtract from view the false self and see only Christ. In those moments when we come to awareness about our attachments, our sin and falsity, we die and are given a glimpse of the One who stands within, waiting to emerge. This same view is then possible to see in others. Coming to awareness about our own baggage, and then moving past it, we can more clearly see that others are in the same condition, that they, too, are Christ, underneath their own layers of falsehood.

The twelfth-century Trappist Bernard of Clairvaux, one of our contemplative tradition's most eloquent voices regarding love, put it this way:

> If you love the Lord your God with all your
> heart, with all your mind, and with all your
> strength,...you will be wholly on fire with the
> fullness of what you have received by the Spirit
> and you will taste God...then you will love
> yourself as you are, since you will know that
> there is nothing to love in you except insofar as
> you are his...you will know yourself as you are, I
> say, when you discover by experience of your love
> of yourself that there is nothing in you worthy of
> love except for his sake, you who without him
> are nothing. As for your neighbor, whom you
> ought to love as yourself: to experience him as
> he is, is the same as to experience yourself, for
> he is as you are.
> ~ *Sermon* 50, III.[6]

---

6 *Bernard of Clairvaux: Selected Works*, trans. G.R. Evans (New York: Paulist, 1987), 244.

The process of coming to the truth about ourselves is sometimes painful. We see our sins, our passionate attachments with numbing clarity. We see their entrenched, habitual nature. This can be discouraging, if we think that our spirituality is all about making ourselves into a better person. It is even more discouraging if we think that detachment is the purposeful effort to "let go" of all those things that we do not like about ourselves.

Things are decidedly different, however, if we see faith as the process of coming to awareness about the false self, humbly standing before God in truth, and allowing divine grace to slowly subtract all that is not real from our beings, so that we can become nothing in ourselves and everything in Christ.

Detachment is the process of becoming nothing and becoming everything. It is the process that leads to true freedom. For Christ's freedom is complete, not like the partial freedom that comes from trying to make ourselves better persons. Detachment is also the process that leads us to true love. For Christ's love is complete and unconditional, not like the partial, conditional love that comes from loving from within our attachments.

Becoming Christ

St. Paul boldly claimed "For freedom Christ has set us free" (Gal. 5:1). This is the aim of the Christian life. We are called into Christ's life, and Christ was nothing if not free. He was free to live without fear, trusting in God's nearness and love. He was free to speak and act according to the direction of the Spirit, without regard for the cost. He was free to live without attachment or anxiety, in complete joy and deep peace. He was free to love everyone without condition, without limit.

We cannot achieve this freedom by wishing it, or by deciding we are going to be that way. We must undergo a journey of transformation; we must die to our false selves and allow Christ's life to resurrect within us. In this journey we become transfigured in Christ's light; we become him, he becomes us. By living in him, we become free in him as he is free. We lose our fear and our idolatrous attachments, we are less enslaved by sin, we learn to live in harmony and equanimity, and we gain a growing sense of gratitude and passion for life.

Contemplative prayer is not the only pathway that leads to this transfiguration. Others journey in a way that is more primarily focused on service, or discursive prayer, or an immersion in the wonder of creation. But contemplative prayer is a reliable pathway, one that will take us, over time, into the freedom of Christ.

This pathway is well-traveled by many pilgrims before us, including the desert mystics who authored Holy Scripture, the fathers and mothers of our theological tradition, medieval monastics, and saints of our own time, who are now showing us the contemplative way "in the world." The contemplative path is balanced by the church's life and worship: through community, service to those in need, the daily offices, the eucharist, the story of scripture and the wisdom of doctrine. The contemplative way encompasses and utilizes our whole being: will, mind, and heart; body, intellect, and spirit. It brings into focus and transforms the pain and difficulty of life.

Through a life that is centered in contemplative practice and awareness, we are led deeply into the mystery of Christ. Dying to all that is false, a new being emerges, one that resembles Jesus of Nazareth. This new being will always retain our personal characteristics, and even elements of our sin, but it will also show forth Jesus' very being. Through us Jesus lives. We are his body, together, all of us. Each of us is a unique individual expression of Jesus' life, and together we make up the whole of him.

At the year 2000 General Convention of the Episcopal Church in Denver, there was on display in the worship hall an enormous banner. From a distance, one could see clearly that it was the image of Christ. As you approached it, what became apparent was that the image was entirely made up of pixels, small photographs of hundreds, perhaps thousands of people: old, young, male, female, black, white, brown, yellow, and red. The only words on the banner were these: *Behold the Face of God.*

We are the body of Christ alive in the world, and he is the human face of God. But to manifest Christ in our lives, to reveal him to the world, we must undergo a journey of transformation by which we become him, and he becomes us. Contemplative prayer, practiced with faith and patience, undertaken in the context of the church's life, takes us on this journey into Christ.

❀

Appendix

A BIBLIOGRAPHY OF PATRISTIC AND EASTERN ORTHODOX SOURCES

There are many wonderful and accessible spiritual authors in our own day, whose voices offer a fresh and modern perspective on the Christian contemplative path. The contemporary style of these authors certainly helps many readers hear what this traditional path has to offer. But there are also many early authors whose wisdom remains unknown to most readers, partly because their works are less available, and partly because their writing is in an ancient voice that comes out of a world quite different than our own.

The early patristic saints form the wellspring of the Christian contemplative perspective. They influenced all that came after them, right down to our own day. They are the ones who speak to me most deeply in my own journey, together with later Eastern Orthodox writers who faithfully preserved and handed down to new generations the patristic contemplative lineage. Steeped in the silence of desert life, their voice is simple, humane, heart-felt, experientially based, psychologically astute, and crystal clear. I have quoted them extensively in this book, and I offer this reading list to those who are interested in pursuing them further.

Primary Patristic Sources
The Sayings of the Desert Fathers, tr. Benedicta Ward (Kalamazoo: Cistercian Publications, 1975). In my view, the best contemporary translation of the *Sayings*, an essential text of the tradition.

Of the other patristic contemplative authors whose writings I am familiar with, the following are the ones whose writings seem to me to be the most understandable to modern ears and directly experiential in nature. The following short list is by no means complete, but it is a good start.

I especially recommend two publishers of these sources, both of which provide very readable and accurate translations, informative historical introductions and helpful notes:

- Paulist Press, Classics in Western Spirituality series
- Cistercian Publications

Origen (185–254)
An Exhortation to Martyrdom, On Prayer

Gregory of Nyssa (332–395)
The Life of Moses, Homilies

Evagrius Ponticus (346–399)
The Praktikos and Chapters on Prayer

John Chrysostom (347–407)
Homilies

Pseudo-Macarius (4th C)
The Fifty Spiritual Homilies and The Great Letter

Augustine of Hippo (354–430)
The Confessions, Homilies

John Cassian (365–435)
The Conferences

Pseudo-Dionysius (5th–6th C)
The Divine Names, Mystical Theology

John Climacus (579–649)
The Ladder of Divine Ascent

Isaac the Syrian (7th C)
Homilies, Mystic Treatises

Patristic Compilations

The Roots of Christian Mysticism, Olivier Clement (Hyde Park: New City Press, 1993). Numerous short selections of all the key patristic sources, linked together thematically with a very readable commentary by an excellent scholar.

Readings for the Daily Office, J. Robert Wright (New York: Church Publishing Inc., 1991). An excellent and thorough collection of short selections from patristic sources, arranged to be used along with the Daily Offices. The readings are carefully chosen to support themes of the appointed readings for the entire liturgical year.

Drinking from the Hidden Fountain: A Patristic Breviary, Thomas Spidlik, tr. Paul Drake (Kalamazoo: Cistercian Publications, 1994). A very good collection, similar to Wright's, but arranged by calendar date and themes chosen by the author, not coordinated with liturgical seasons and daily readings.

A Compilation of Patristic and Eastern Orthodox Authors (4th-14thC)

The Philokalia, The Complete Text, Vol. I–IV, tr. G.E.H. Palmer, Philip Sherrard, Kallistos Ware (London: Faber and Faber, 1979, 1981, 1984, 1995). This classic and historically essential series is being translated into English from the original Greek, published in 1782 by Nikodimos of the Holy Mountain and Makarios of Corinth. The English version will be finalized when the fifth volume comes out. This is the most complete and respected collection of authors from the 1600-year-old patristic and Eastern tradition of contemplative practice and theology.

The complete *Philokalia* in English was preceded by a one-volume collection entitled *Writings from the Philokalia on Prayer of the Heart*, tr. E. Kadloubovsky and GEH Palmer (London: Faber and Faber, 1951). This collection was taken from Theophan the Recluse's 19th C Russian version (entitled *Dobrotolubiye*) of Nikodimos' and Makarios' 18th C *Philokalia*. *Writings from the Philokalia on Prayer of the Heart* is probably the best place to start reading from the *Philokalia*.

A 19th C Russian Compilation
The Art of Prayer: An Orthodox Anthology, compiled by Igumen Chariton, trans. E. Kadloubovsky and E.M. Palmer, ed. Timothy Ware (London: Faber and Faber, 1966). A beautiful collection of passages from 19th C Russian authors on the Jesus Prayer/Prayer of the Heart (principally Theophan the Recluse, 1815–1894).

The Jesus Prayer
The Way of a Pilgrim, Anonymous, trans. R.M. French (San Francisco: HarperSanFrancisco,1991).

The Jesus Prayer, by a Monk of the Eastern Church (Crestwood: St. Vladimir's Seminary Press, 1997). Probably the simplest, most informative, practical and readable text available on the Jesus Prayer.

BECOMING CHRIST